*The
End
Battle*

Also by Corrie ten Boom

Amazing Love
Clippings from My Notebook: Writings and
    Sayings Collected by Corrie ten Boom
Common Sense Not Needed: Some
    Thoughts about an Unappreciated
    Work among Neglected People
Corrie's Christmas Memories
Corrie ten Boom's Prison Letters
Don't Wrestle, Just Nestle
Each New Day
Father ten Boom: God's Man
He Cares, He Comforts
He Sets the Captives Free
The Hiding Place
In My Father's House: The Years before
    "The Hiding Place"
Jesus Is Victor
Not Good if Detached
Not I, but Christ
Plenty for Everyone
Prayers and Promises for Every Day
A Prisoner and Yet . . .
This Day Is the Lord's
A Tramp Finds a Home
Tramp for the Lord

The
End
Battle

Corrie ten Boom

Fleming H. Revell
A Division of Baker Book House
Grand Rapids, Michigan 49516

Published by Fleming H. Revell
a division of Baker Book House Company
P.O. Box 6287, Grand Rapids, MI 49516-6287

Parts 1–4 originally published as *Marching Orders for the End Battle*
(1969); part 5 originally published as *Defeated Enemies* (1962)

First printing, September 1997

Printed in the United States of America

Library of Congress Cataloging-in-Publication Data

Ten Boom, Corrie.
  [Marching orders for the end battle]
  The end battle / Corrie ten Boom.
    p.   cm.
  "Parts 1–4 originally published as Marching orders for the end
battle (1969); part 5 originally published as Defeated enemies
(1962)"—T.p. verso.
    ISBN 0-8007-1743-0 (cloth)
    1. Christian life. I. Ten Boom, Corrie. Defeated enemies.
II. Title. III. Title: Defeated enemies.
BV4501.2.3825   1997
243—dc21   97-11032

Unless otherwise indicated,
Scripture quotations are from
the King James Version of the
Bible.

Scripture quotations identified
ANT are from the Amplified ®
New Testament. Copyright
© 1954, 1958 by the Lockman
Foundation. Used by permission.

Scripture quotations identified LB
are from *The Living Bible* © 1971.
Used by permission of Tyndale
House Publishers, Inc., Wheaton,
IL 60189. All rights reserved.

Scripture quotations identified
NEB are from *The New English
Bible.* Copyright © 1961, 1970,
1989 by The Delegates of Oxford
University Press and The Syndics
of the Cambridge University
Press. Reprinted by permission.

Scripture quotations identified
PHILLIPS are from *The New Testa-
ment in Modern English* by J. B.
Phillips. © 1958 by J. B. Phillips.

Scripture quotations identified
RSV are from the Revised Stan-
dard Version of the Bible, copyright 1946, 1952 by the Division
of Christian Education of the
National Council of the Churches
of Christ in the USA. Used by
permission.

For current information about all
releases from Baker Book House,
visit our web site:
    http://www.bakerbooks.com

Contents

Preface

In Vietnam I met a man from the jungle: Tsau. He came to me after I had spoken five times to his Chil tribe. He said, "Double old grandmother." Just imagine being called such a thing when you are only seventy-five years old, but to be old is the greatest honor in the Chil tribe; he wanted to say something really flattering. "You came from far, far away to tell us about Jesus. You traveled long, very long; you are old, very old. Will you thank your tribe in the name of our Chil tribe that they allowed you to come to us? We will establish a covenant, a covenant of prayer. You pray for us, we pray for you."

"Tsau, have you a special message for our tribe?" He waited a moment; I believe he prayed. "Yes, tell the people of your tribe that they have to turn away from their sins and repent, so that they may see Jesus when He comes again."

Was Tsau right? Sure, we have to repent and be converted, but also we must prepare for Jesus' coming again.

We believe that in our day we can see clearly the outlines of biblical prophecies in world history. It is good to compare the newspapers with the Bible at this time. Then we understand that Jesus may come very soon. Before His return there will be a hard battle, and therefore it is good to prepare ourselves and to gird our loins with power. Every Christian is called to take his place in the army of King Jesus and to wrestle as a fellow conqueror with Him. "For we wrestle not against flesh and blood, but against principalities, against powers . . . against spiritual wickedness in high places" (Eph. 6:12).

This battle is more violent than ever before. The devil knows that his time is short. Everything is heading toward the great and final battle which John describes in the Book of Revelation, and that battle has started already. But we know:

> Jesus was Victor.
> Jesus is Victor.
> Jesus will be Victor.

PART 1

Marching Orders

1
Stimulation to Militancy

God's plans for the victory are perfect. He knows the enemy and the reactions of the enemy before the foundation of the world and He does not need to fear any unexpected attack. He also knows His men. He knows their need for food and clothing. He provides the equipment and He launches them at the right time and the right place, for He leads them to victory. Those who fight on our side are greater and stronger than those who stand against us: We have a mighty High Priest and legions of angels. Jesus came to destroy the works of the devil. At the cross of Calvary He has already won the victory. There He crushed the head of the serpent. Above all things we need to know our position in this battle. The Bible speaks of this position: to be hid with Christ in God. What a comfort to know that we belong to the victorious army of God, when we look at the seemingly superior forces of the enemy. Nowadays there are many atheistic ideologies. The enemy also uses Marxism in the form of communism to persuade mankind that God does not exist. There are many people who are fervent communists.

Once I read a testimony of a communist. He wrote:

> We are fanatics. Our lives are absorbed by one tremendous all-important factor: the battle for world-communism. We communists would not spend any money on concerts or other pleasures. We have set a clear aim before our eyes. We have an ideal to fight for. We dedicate ourselves and our personal lives and possessions in the service of a great movement. What does it matter that our personal lives, our own egos have to suffer for the sake of the party? We are fully rewarded at the thought that every one of us is co-operating a little in the creation of something new, something better for mankind. There is only one thing for which I will die: communism. That is my life. That is my faith, my hobby, my love, my beloved; that is my master, my food and my drink.

During the day I work for it and during the night I dream about it. As time goes on, its influence on me gets stronger and stronger. That's why I cannot make friends, why I cannot love, or even hold a conversation without touching on all this, and this force that stimulates and leads me. I have been in prison for the sake of my ideas, my ideals, and I am willing, if need be, to stand in front of the firing squad.

I know for myself, that it is not just one or a few who think and feel like that. There are hundreds of thousands who have perhaps never said it, but who live in the same manner. We must realize this very clearly. When you take the map of the world, you can see how many countries are under the control of communism and the influence of atheism which is connected with it. When I look at world history in the light of God's Word, then I do not believe that we can expect better times. Politics have no answer for this progress of atheism. Someone has said: "We have reached in our history of civilization the point where the most serious crisis starts that mankind has ever experienced."

That is true; there is a great battle going on in the invisible world. It is easy to believe what Peter writes; it seems to be an even greater reality now than in those days: "Be sober, be vigilant; because your adversary the devil, as a roaring lion, walketh about, seeking whom he may devour: whom resist steadfast in the faith, knowing that the same afflictions are accomplished in your brethren that are in the world" (1 Peter 5:8–9).

Every Christian is involved in this battle, whether he wants it or not. The enemy will try with all his might to alienate us from God, to destroy our faith in Jesus Christ, and to make us rebellious against God. We can shut our eyes to the danger and not see where the course of world history will lead us. But Jesus says in Luke 21:36: "Watch ye therefore, and pray always, that ye may be accounted worthy to escape all these things that shall come to pass, and to stand before the Son of man."

In this time there are two sorts of people who are important: the fully dedicated children of God and the fully dedicated atheists. Every Christian is called to be involved in this fight. You can decide for yourself if you will be a good, a mediocre, or a bad wrestler. Jesus Himself transforms everyone who surrenders fully to Him into a warrior led by the Holy Spirit, a warrior who looks forward to the final victory when Jesus comes again. Such a person has a strong case against the enemy and is never ashamed of his King.

This is the work of the Holy Spirit. He gives us a vision of the final victory of Jesus Christ. "That is why God has now lifted him so high, and has given him the name beyond all names, so that at the name of Jesus 'every knee shall bow,' whether in Heaven or earth or under the earth. And that is why, in the end, 'every tongue shall confess' that Jesus Christ is the Lord, to the glory of God the Father" (Phil. 2:9–11 PHILLIPS).

The Holy Sprit will prepare us: "He which hath begun a good work in you will perform it until the day of Jesus Christ" (Phil. 1:6).

2
Be Prepared

~~~~~

Atheism is expanding. The kingdom of God is going on quietly. Now it is either-or; Christ or Antichrist. Nobody can serve two masters; either the one or the other. The divisions are becoming clear-cut. We have this great comfort, that God has shown us that He has a plan for this world. He has no problems, only plans. That is why there is never a panic in heaven. Knowing the future gives us strength and security.

For God has allowed us to know the secret of his plan, and it is this: he purposes in his sovereign will that all human history shall be consummated in Christ, that everything that exists in Heaven or earth shall find its perfection and fulfillment in him. And here is the staggering thing— that in all which will one day belong to him we have been promised a share (since we were long ago destined for this by the

16

one who achieves his purposes by his sovereign will).

Ephesians 1:9–11 PHILLIPS

An abundant richness of strength is at
our disposal. We need this strength. Let us
then be conscious of it in our way of living.
This richness does not depend on circumstances. We must realize this fully, because
circumstances will be difficult in the final
battle. But we shall never lack anything.

Bishop Dzao of China sounded a warning to us when he spoke in the Congress of
Evangelists in Berlin. He said: "China now
experiences what probably will come over
the whole world. Yes, there will come a time
when nobody can buy or sell without the
mark of the Antichrist" (Rev. 13:17).

The Bishop has confessed that the church
in China had not prepared the Christians
for the terrible trials they have to face now.
"We gave them everything we could—the
gospel, churches, yes, food and clothing
where poverty reigned. But one thing we
did not do. We neglected to teach them how
to pass on the gospel to other people. Now
all the preachers and bishops have gone—
the church practically does not exist any-
more. Yes, an invisible church is going on,

but how few Christians were strong enough to strengthen others!" This bishop appealed to us to do our utmost to prepare the children of God in this time and to show them the special task for this time, so that they will be strong enough in the time of oppression. Is it possible that weak little people can be ready for that? Yes, everyone can be ready. I mean what I say. The Lord has given us all we need for the end-time.

"But ye shall receive power, after that the Holy Ghost is come upon you: and ye shall be witnesses unto me both in Jerusalem, and in all Judaea, and in Samaria, and unto the uttermost part of the earth" (Acts 1:8). This was a promise for the time when the church of Jesus Christ came into existence, but these words have never lost their power. Especially in the final battle this promise will be a source of strength for the children of God so that they can lead a victorious life. This power is available, because the Holy Spirit has come and He longs to fill our hearts as the light flows into a room when it is opened to let the daylight in. Be filled with the Holy Spirit! Give room to the Holy Spirit! That means: Surrender!

3
Hope for Sinners

———— ◆◆◆◆ ————

"Ye are the light of the world" (Matt. 5:14). I spoke on this text in a prison. Perhaps you think it is a strange text for murderers and thieves, but I have seen that God can use "good" and "bad" people. I know many evangelists who are still serving their time in prison. The Holy Spirit has convicted them of sin, of righteousness, and of judgment; and in His love for sinners the Lord Jesus has saved them, and made them children of God. I know many who have become real soul-winners, who have led many of their fellow prisoners to the Lord. When I had finished my address, one of the prisoners got up and said: "Friends, today I read in the Bible about three murderers; one was Moses, one was David, one was Paul. We know them all as heroes of faith, but still they have been murderers. What God can do with a murderer who surrenders fully to Him! Fellows, there is also hope for us."

Yes, there is hope for every decent and indecent sinner, when he surrenders to Jesus, when he confesses his sins, when he gets converted by His strength, when he is cleansed by the blood of Jesus and filled with the Holy Spirit. Then he will become the light of the world. There is no sin too great to bring to Jesus. He said: "Come unto me, all." And those who come to Jesus, He will never cast out. The very beginning is this: to come to Jesus and in His strength to turn away from sin. Then one is cleansed and sanctified. And thus, by the power of the Holy Spirit, one becomes through Jesus Christ more than conqueror. Then all fear for the future goes. Then we know that what Paul says in Romans 8:31–39 (PHILLIPS) is true. I have experienced it:

> If God is for us, who can be against us? He who did not shield his own Son but gave him up for us all—can we not trust such a God to give us, with him, everything else that we can need?
>
> Who would dare to accuse us, whom God has chosen? The judge himself has declared us free from sin. Who is in a position to condemn? Only Christ, and Christ

died for us, Christ rose for us, Christ reigns in power for us, Christ prays for us!

Can anything separate us from the love of Christ? Can trouble, pain or persecution? Can lack of clothes and food, danger to life and limb, the threat of force of arms? Indeed some of us know the truth of that ancient text:

> For thy sake we are killed all the day
> long;
> We were accounted as sheep for the
> slaughter.

No, in all these things we win an overwhelming victory through him who has proved his love for us.

I have become absolutely convinced that neither death nor life, neither messenger of Heaven nor monarch of earth, neither what happens today nor what may happen tomorrow, neither a power from on high nor a power from below, nor anything else in God's whole world has any power to separate us from the love of God in Jesus Christ our Lord!

Hallelujah!

4
Training

A soldier must obey. He cannot serve the king and the nation if he does his own will. Jesus was obedient. He, the Creator of the world, always submitted to His Father's will. He set His face toward Jerusalem to be crucified. He was obedient unto the death of the cross. That was His way to the resurrection. This is also the way for His followers, for only the way of obedience, the way of crucifixion, leads to the resurrection. Cross-bearing in the form of martyrdom has become unknown in Western Europe; in Eastern Europe it is not. Nevertheless it is of great importance nowadays, for the opposition against God and the cross is increasing. What can we expect, when atheism will find its climax in the coming and the revelation of the Antichrist?

> That day will not come before there arises
> a definite rejection of God and the appear-
> ance of the lawless man. He is the prod-
> uct of all that leads to death, and he sets
> himself up in opposition to every religion.
>
> 2 Thessalonians 2:3–4 PHILLIPS

Will God be defeated? No. After this period of darkness, His trumpet will sound and His Son Jesus Christ will come. Then it will be very clearly manifested that the gospel is brought indeed to all nations. "Go ye therefore, and make disciples of all the nations" is the command.

Once a woman read in her Bible during the morning hour from 1 Thessalonians 4:16–18 (PHILLIPS):

> One word of command, one shout from
> the Archangel, one blast from the trum-
> pet of God and the Lord himself will come
> down from Heaven! Those who have died
> in Christ will be the first to arise, and, we
> who are still living on the earth will be
> swept up with them into the clouds to
> meet the Lord in the air. And after that we
> shall be with Him for ever.
>
> God has given me this message on the
> matter, so by all means use it to encour-
> age one another.

When she read this, her thoughts were fixed particularly on the seriousness of this passage. The signs of the times are clear and everyone knows that great events are coming. Not only Bible readers know this, but also the people who read the newspapers. She was so completely taken up in meditating about Jesus' coming, that she did not hear the doorbell ring. After some time she suddenly heard it and opened the door quickly, her Bible still in her hand.

"It seems as if you are becoming deaf, lady! I had to ring the bell three times!" the milkman said.

"Oh, I am so sorry. No, I am not deaf, but I was reading something in the Bible that was so great, that I forgot everything around me. Do you know, it is possible that one day you will come to my door and I will not be here? And everywhere you ring the bell where Christians used to live, you will find the houses empty. I just read that when Jesus comes again, we will meet Him in the air. Then we shall be suddenly changed and we shall see Him face to face. You would not understand why so many people had suddenly disappeared. Later on you would hear what had happened and then you would ask why that old lady had not told you that before. And that's why I tell you now. Listen, milkman, when you accept Jesus as your Savior, then you will become a child of God too, and will belong to those who will meet Him in the air."

Whether we agree with the point of view of this old lady or not, we notice that she really meant what she said, and that she looked forward to the coming again of Jesus. It is not at all important whether we have much money at this time. But it is very important that at that moment other people will go with us to meet the Lord, people to whom we showed the way of salvation.

The armor of God in Ephesians 6 is not solely described as the armor of the soldiers of Jesus Christ in the victorious final battle, but also for the time of Paul as well as for this time. Because we know that the great final battle will start soon, this armor and absolute obedience to the marching orders in these last days are very important. Jesus said in Luke 21:8 that these days would come, and we can see already from the newspapers that they are upon us. Let us not be afraid; these things must happen first.

It is so kind of the Lord to tell us this beforehand. We are, strictly speaking, the only people in the whole world who know the future and who understand the present time. This knowledge does not need to make us downhearted, because the Lord has spoken many comforting words in view of the future: "But there shall not a hair of your head perish. In your patience possess ye your souls. . . . And when these things begin to come to pass, then look up, and lift up your heads; for your redemption draweth nigh. . . . So likewise ye, when ye see these things come to pass, know ye that the kingdom of God is nigh at hand" (Luke 21:18–19, 28, 31).

It is important to persevere in this time; then we can go through life with uplifted head, our eyes fixed on Jesus. The moment comes that we shall see the Son of man coming on a cloud with great power and glory. All these perspectives we know through God's Word. "I will hasten my word to perform it" (Jer. 1:12). "Heaven and earth shall pass away, but my words shall not pass away" (Matt. 24:35). "Watch ye therefore, and pray always, that ye may be accounted worthy to escape all these things that shall come to pass . . ." (Luke 21:36). "Be on your guard—see to it that your minds are never clouded by dissipation or drunkenness or the worries of this life, or else that day may catch you like the springing of a trap" (Luke 21:34 PHILLIPS).

Worries of this life, we all know them! Is that, then, wrong? No, but they can occupy us, and that day would come upon us as a terrible surprise, because we forgot to be vigilant and had not prepared ourselves for it. So it was also in the time of the deluge:

> For just as life went on in the days of Noah so will it be at the coming of the Son of Man. In those days before the Flood people were eating, drinking, marrying and being given in marriage until the very day that Noah went into the Ark, and knew nothing about the Flood until it came and destroyed them all. So will it be at the coming of the Son of Man.
>
> Matthew 24:37–39 PHILLIPS

Everywhere in the world there are children of God who have difficulties, especially those who really mean business with the Word of God and with their call to be the light of the world and the salt of the earth. Very often their fellow Christians make it hard for them because they do not agree with some biblical truths and because they cannot accept the total surrender with all its consequences. In these difficulties, one must practice patience and love. The devil likes it when we, like iconoclasts, ruthlessly throw away old truths and traditions. "If I have the gift of foretelling the future and hold in my mind not only all human knowledge but the very secrets of God, and if I also have that absolute faith which can move mountains, but have no love, I amount to nothing at all" (1 Cor. 13:2 PHILLIPS).

When the devil cannot keep us back, he tries to push us so fast that we exaggerate. Then we are in danger of forgetting to love. It is very important for us to understand that all these temptations and trials belong to training for the final battle. The "trainer," the Holy Spirit, gives us what we need. He teaches us to be patient, to look at the Lord, to pay attention to our fellow warriors, and not to burden ourselves with superfluous luggage. This is all a part of the victorious life; while He trains conquerors, He comforts us with His bountiful promises.

PART 2

Conquerors

5
Victory over Sins in Daily Life

We must have clear vision, but our sins often hinder us. They confuse our sight. Therefore it is so important that we are obedient to the command of the Lord: "Everyone who has at heart a hope like that keeps himself pure, for he knows how pure Christ is" (1 John 3:3 PHILLIPS).

He who waits for Jesus' coming again becomes sensitive to every shadow that comes between his Master and himself, and he does not rest until the vision is clear again. We must understand clearly that this text does not mean a striving to make ourselves better and better. We must look at Jesus, our hope. He is the Lord, who sanctifies us. The Holy Spirit gives us what we need.

"The Spirit . . . produces in human life fruits such as these: love, joy, peace, patience, kindness, generosity, fidelity, tolerance and self-control" (Gal. 5:22 PHILLIPS).

The devil accuses us night and day. He likes to push us into dismay, because then we cannot be strong. But the Word of God says to us: "Be strong in the Lord." He can give us this command, because He Himself gives us His strength. As soon as we realize that there is a sin in our hearts, we must bring it to the Lord, because that sin makes us insecure and weak. We must know that it is really true that the blood of Jesus cleanses us from all sins we bring to Him. When we confess our sins, He is faithful and just to forgive us our sins (1 John 1:7, 9). When we confess our sins to the Lord and ask for forgiveness, He will cast them into the depths of the sea. "He will turn again, he will have compassion upon us; he will subdue our iniquities; and thou wilt cast all their sins into the depths of the sea" (Micah 7:19).

He will forgive and forget, and I believe that He sometimes must put up a little sign: "No fishing allowed!" This is necessary, because sin confessed to the Lord is gone. At the cross Jesus finished everything. "For our fight is not against any physical enemy: it is against organizations and powers that are spiritual" (Eph. 6:12 PHILLIPS). "Your enemy the devil is always about, prowling like a lion roaring for its prey" (1 Peter 5:8 PHILLIPS).

When we think of the future, when the great final battle takes place, we can very well imagine roaring lions and evil spirits, but we must not forget that these are now already mobilized in the battle and it is part of our training that we recognize them and become firm. The devil is like a lion, but he is chained up. When we do not come too close, we are not in danger. I remember a friend who had to fight against a bad temper. Having tempers is in the eyes of many people a decent sin, but in reality it is a horrible sin, which gives the people around us very much sorrow and suffering. That friend longed with all his heart for victory over that sin. Then someone gave him this advice: "You must take care that you do not come too close to the lion! Don't forget that he is chained up!" Jesus tied him to a chain: He came to conquer the devil and to break the works of the devil. Yes, the children of God are attacked much at this very time and it is good to know our enemy; that is why it is necessary to be victor now in daily life and to surrender completely to the Lord

Jesus. Jesus is always Conqueror! All we
have to do is to see to it that we remain in
good contact with Him and then His life of
victory will flow through us and touch the
people around us. Our everyday life is our
battle place. A part of God's strategy is to
appoint the place where we have to fight.
We cannot escape the war by looking for
another front line. Our place with Him is
here, under His banner of the cross! Jonah
was disobedient and wanted to run away
from his call, but one can never hide himself from God (Jonah 1:3).

Are you sure that you are in the place
where you are called? In the office, at the
engine, at the side of your husband or wife?
Jesus gives you your place. "Abide in me,"
He says, "and I in you. As the branch cannot bear fruit of itself, except it abide in the
vine; no more can ye, except ye abide in me"
(John 15:4). Your place is in Him. There is
no room and no time for our own plans to
do private battle with the evil one, for a
game with the chained-up lion, for coquet-
ting with great or small sins of everyday life.
With Jesus hid in God! Can we find a safer
hiding place? The devil will have to go first
through God and Jesus before he reaches
us! When soldiers are trained, they receive

their training in barracks together with others. The training in the victorious army of God for the last great battle does not take place under unusual circumstances, but in the midst of the common daily life. Here is the place of training—and everything we experience belongs to that training. So do our contacts with our fellow men. In the first letter of Peter we read that all difficulties and temptations work together to get us prepared:

> This means tremendous joy to you, I know, even though at present you are temporarily harassed by all kinds of trials and temptations. This is no accident—it happens to prove your faith, which is infinitely more valuable than gold, and gold as you know, even though it is ultimately perishable, must be purified by fire. This proving of your faith is planned to bring you praise and honor and glory in the day when Jesus Christ reveals himself.
>
> 1 Peter 1:6–7 PHILLIPS

You are encouraged when you see the temptations of everyday life in that light. It can be difficult, but when you see it from God's point of view, then you know that the greatest power of God's love and joy, the fruit of the Holy Spirit, is at our disposal in daily life. What a mystery! When things are seen from the viewpoint of eternity, it makes you patient, for you know: "I am like gold that must be purified." Then you will fix your eyes upward—and you do this again and again.

6
Victory through Decreasing

~~~~~

Do you ever have days when everything goes wrong? You try to do your utmost, but you do not succeed at all. I remember one week in which every day was more mixed up than the day before. First everything seemed to go so well. I was to work eight days in a town in Australia. A minister there had invited me as his guest in his home. Although he had many children, he could make room for me.

When you travel a great deal, it is always difficult if you have nowhere to unpack your suitcase. It was a very dark small room in which I would have to live that week. I could not hang up my clothes. I had no table to write at. But you get used to these difficulties. When things are very bad I always say: "Lord Jesus, You have had times when You had nowhere to lay Your head. I am in Your service. This is just a little bit of cross-bearing."

But the little room was not the worst problem. The minister was difficult to work with. When we talked about the plans for the week, I was not allowed to make any decision by myself. He just dictated everything I had to do; and I did try to be obedient. When he told me that he had to preach the gospel in a mental hospital, I became quite enthusiastic. "Can I go with you and work there too?"

"Oh," he said, and looked at me very unkindly, "you, a woman? Well, all right; why not? If you would like to do that, we can organize something." But after the first meeting in his church, I felt that we did not form a team at all. His ideas were so different from mine, it was difficult to cooperate with him.

After three days, I became frightened to go with this man, with whom I was not united in spirit at all, to a place where so often there are many powers of darkness. I decided to speak to him about this. I went to his study and said: "Pastor, I believe that I cannot go to that institution. We ought to be closely united as a team and we are not."

He became angry. "You have said that you wanted to go, and now you must go!" I refused. "You must; you have to do what I tell you."

I got up and went to the garden. I had a real, inward struggle. I was offended. I was afraid. What right had this man to dictate what I had to do? But then I understood; I had to decrease still more. Someone who has lost his life for Jesus' sake cannot be offended! I prayed: "Lord, You know that I cannot do this, but I will go the lowest way. Must I do what this man says and go with him to the institution? I am afraid of it, Lord! But I will go the way of obedience."

It took a full hour before peace came into my heart. Then I went back to the study. "Pastor, if you say that I have to go, then I will do it."

His answer settled the matter. "Oh no; it is not necessary to go. I phoned the director of the institution and told him that you would not come."

"Oh, Pastor, how glad I am!"

"Yes, it was not difficult at all. I simply said to him: 'This Corrie ten Boom has been in a concentration camp for a time. Now she is not quite normal; we must just accept that!'"

I turned away and went to my little room. Yes, it was a relief that I did not have to go to that mental hospital, but how offended I was!

And so I had to be on the platform with this man for another four days. People came to visit me, but they were not allowed to do so. I almost lost courage, and I was afraid that it would become a lost week.

There was always a young Baptist minister with members of his congregation in the meetings. He always listened with an open heart. It is a joy to have someone in a meeting who by the expression on his face gives you a "real answer." That gave me a bit more confidence. The last evening was perhaps the most difficult of all. I spoke about full surrender, about walking in the light as Jesus is in the light, so that we can have fellowship one with the other—but I felt that I had no fellowship with my host, and also that I did not walk in the light with him. The Baptist pastor said to me: "I can take you to your next place tonight by car. It is about three hundred miles away from here, but I am used to driving by night. When I was a student I worked for my brother as a driver on his truck, and always had to drive during the night. While I am taking you

there, we can be talking. Will you be sure
that your luggage is ready?"

That was a lovely suggestion. That evening
I felt I spoke with authority, although everything was difficult. I humbled myself before
the people without telling them what had
been my greatest problem during the whole
week. When I told my host I would leave at
eleven o'clock that night and that the Baptist pastor would take me to the next place,
he was furious. "I will take you myself tomorrow!" he said. But I knew that I had to do my
own will now.

At eleven o'clock I went out of the front
door with my luggage and I found the Baptist minister there. That nocturnal journey
was a joy. It was a present from the Lord.
The minister told me what had happened
in his congregation: "There were so many
disagreements, so much hatred, that the
Holy Spirit must have been very grieved
with such a congregation, but almost all the
members of my church have been in your
meetings every evening and the Lord has
worked! Tonight everything was altered.
After the meeting we all stood outside, because we were not allowed to stay inside,
and there we prayed together. People who
have not been speaking to each other for

years have now been reconciled. They have confessed their sins, and they have put everything right. What happened there in front of the church was such a blessing that we know we can now start afresh with our whole congregation. We praise and thank the Lord that He brought you here. He used the whole week."

So it had not been wrong as I had feared. It had been difficult, but not for nothing! We had a joyful journey that dark night. From time to time he stopped the car and we had a time of prayer. I confessed my sin before the Lord. I wanted to start the work in the next place cleansed and sanctified. I had to confess to the Lord that I had been hurt in my pride, that I had had self-pity, that I was discouraged and had a critical spirit in my heart. The spirit of sorrow had been on the throne. What a joy to bring everything to the Lord, because when we confess our sins, He is faithful and just to forgive us our sins and the blood of Jesus cleanses us from all sins! This experience had been an exercise to get smaller. I had made a mistake when, in my enthusiasm, I offered too quickly to go to that mental institution. We must not make plans if we are not in the presence of the Lord. That is why prayer time gives the best atmosphere to plan a program.

Once I read a legend: Peter and the other disciples of Jesus went with the Lord on a long journey. Everything went too slowly for Peter and he walked on alone. Then he came to a road where it was dangerous because of wild animals and robbers. Peter found himself in danger. He hid behind a rock and waited until the others came. Then he said to Jesus: "I was afraid; I was in danger. There are wild animals and robbers here." Jesus looked at him very kindly and said: "Peter, you must never go ahead of Me. You must always remain by My side, then you are safe."

7

*Victory through
the Blood of Jesus*

―――――― ∞∞∞∞ ――――――

"Now they have conquered him through the blood of the Lamb, and through the Word to which they bore witness. They did not cherish life even in the face of death!" (Rev. 12:11 PHILLIPS). Yes, the blood of Jesus Christ has great power!

There is perhaps not a word in the Bible that is so full of secret truths as the blood of Jesus. It is the secret of His incarnation, when Jesus took our flesh and blood; the secret of His obedience unto death, when He gave His blood at the cross of Calvary; the secret of His love that went beyond all understanding, when He bought us with His blood; the secret of His victory over the enemy; and the secret of our eternal salvation. Why does the devil hate this word? Because it reminds him of his defeat on Calvary by the death of Jesus who gave His blood for us, but also because it reminds him of Jesus, the resurrected One, to whom we always may come with our sins. That is why the devil is afraid of it. The blood of Jesus Christ has great power.

Once I visited a big prison in Manila. It was a hotbed of sin. There were seven thousand prisoners. I had an opportunity to speak there during three afternoons and when I entered I noticed that above the door was written: "Security limit." I asked what that meant and was told that when anyone entered this prison he had to go at his own risk in the midst of a big group of criminals, because there were only a very few guards. I looked into my heart to see if I was afraid— and yes, I must admit that indeed there was much fear! But, what could I do? I knew that I was in the way of the Lord, so I had to obey! When I came to the inner court, a great surprise was waiting for me: There was a band of musicians of about ninety men! When they saw me, they started to play: "There is power, power, wonder-working power in the precious blood of the Lamb!" All my fear disappeared. There is no reason to be afraid when a child of God is under the protection of the blood of the Lamb, the blood of Jesus. God gave us a very great blessing. Three times I reached seven thousand men with the help of a loudspeaker. I reached them with the rich gospel, the glad tidings for sinners.

8
Victory through the Name of Jesus

~~~~~

The name of Jesus is wonderful! Once I heard a story of a sick lady in Germany. A friend asked her: "Do you know it is written in the Bible that Jesus said: 'They will lay their hands upon the sick and they will recover'?" Then he read Mark 16 and asked: "Do you believe the Bible?"

"Yes," she said, "I believe the whole Bible."

Then he simply did it. In the name of Jesus he laid his hands on her and she was healed.

She was so happy that she went to her pastor and said: "Did you know that that text in Mark 16:18 is in the Bible?"

The pastor's answer was: "I am so sorry, but I must tell you that that part of Mark 16 was added to the Bible long, long afterwards."

One moment she was very disappointed, but suddenly her eyes started to beam with joy and she said: "What a wonderful Book is the Bible, that even an added promise has so much power that I was healed!"

Yes, when we believe the rich treasures of the Bible, we experience that God, who gave us all these promises, really keeps them. The name of Jesus is a wonderful name. The Bible does not only teach us that we *can* pray in this name, but that we *should* pray in Jesus' name. Once I heard a very good example of this from my friend William Nagenda, an African brother. He told me about a letter that his wife wrote him when he was abroad. Their little boy, age three, asked: "Mummy, what are you doing?"

"I am writing a letter to daddy."

"I will write a letter to daddy too."

She gave him a piece of paper and a pencil and then he made all kinds of scrawls. "This is my letter to daddy," the boy said. The mother wrote under all these scrawls: "This is Christopher's letter to his daddy."

When William took this letter from the envelope, he first wanted to throw it away, but then he saw what was written on it:

"This is Christopher's letter to his daddy."
Suddenly he felt very proud and he asked
his friend: "Have you a boy of three?"

"Yes."

"Has he ever written you a letter?"

"No, of course not."

"My son has written me a letter," and he
showed him the paper with all the scrawls.
He was very proud. Why did he set so much
value on that letter? Because his wife had
explained what those scrawls meant.

When we pray, it doesn't matter whether
it is a beautiful prayer, or a prayer from our
prayer book, or perhaps just a cry of distress
directed to the Lord. It is never good
enough for the holy God; but when we say:
"In the name of Jesus," then it is just as if
Jesus says: "Father, this is a prayer from
your child, Mary, John, Charles . . . ," and
then the heavenly Father is delighted with
our prayer! That prayer is sanctified by the
name of Jesus. Therefore, use this name!
Not the name "Christ"; that is His title. The
name that is above every name in heaven
or on earth is the name Jesus, Savior! He is
our strength. "In no one else can salvation
be found. For in all the world no other name
has been given to men but this, and it is by

this name that we must be saved!" (Acts 4:12 PHILLIPS).

That name brings heaven and earth together. One cannot overestimate the value of that name in the great final battle.

9

Victory through the Holy Spirit

〜〜〜

"You are to be given power when the Holy Spirit has come to you. You will be witnesses to me, not only in Jerusalem, not only throughout Judaea, not only in Samaria, but to the very ends of the earth!" (Acts 1:8 PHILLIPS). This power of the Holy Spirit is of tremendous value to us. The Bible says: "Be filled with the Spirit!" In Haarlem lives a woman who started a prayer meeting in her room. Her brother had not much faith about it and said: "You will never succeed!" But the day after, she told him: "My room was full up!"

"All right, but just wait and see what happens next week!"

But the next time she said: "My room was even fuller." And the third time: "Now it was fuller still!"

Her brother said: "That is impossible; when your room is full, it cannot be fuller."

"Oh, yes," she said. "Every week we took some more furniture out of the room."

When we are filled with the Holy Spirit, then another step may be necessary. It is possible that some furniture must be removed from the heart: television, some books, friendships, personal hobbies, everything that can hinder us from following Jesus Christ. We can clear out still more for Jesus, so that we can give more room to the Holy Spirit. My glove cannot do anything by itself, but when my hand is in the glove, it can do a great deal. It can even cook, write, and do many things! I know that it is not the glove, but the hand in the glove. When I put only one finger in the glove, then it cannot do anything! So it is with us. We are gloves; the Holy Spirit is the hand which can do everything, but we must give Him room right into the outer corners of our lives. Then we can expect that He can do a lot in and through us. In John 14:17 it is written: "He is with you now and will be in your hearts" (PHILLIPS). "So, if you, for all your evil, know how to give good things to your children, how much more likely is it that your Heavenly Father will

give the Holy Spirit to those who ask him!"
(Luke 11:13 PHILLIPS).

John the Baptist had said already: "The
one who comes after me . . . will baptize
you with the Holy Spirit and with fire"
(Matt. 3:11 NEB). Jesus is the Baptizer in
the Holy Spirit and therefore the fullness
of the Holy Spirit is the birthright of every
child of God.

Gifts of the Spirit

A missionary in China had to endure brain-
washing. He resisted and fought against it,
but the moment came when he felt he was
at the end of his strength. Then he started
to pray in tongues. That fellowship with the
Lord, in absolute relaxation, was his salvation. The enemy could not influence his
mind any longer. I believe that the Lord has
given this gift at this time to many of His
children in many different churches and
groups, because it is a strong weapon and
will prove to be so in the final battle. It is a
fact that nothing has received so much criticism and opposition, even among believing
Christians, as has this gift, which is described
so clearly in the Word of God. Paul says in
1 Corinthians 14:5: "I should indeed like you

all to speak with 'tongues'" (PHILLIPS). The "God is dead" theology and occultism, which are practiced even by Christians, receive less criticism and resistance, yes, and even enmity, than this gift from the Spirit. Mother Basilea, the leader of the "Sisters of Mary" in Darmstadt, has said:

"We need the fullness of the Holy Spirit for the end-time, which is the period in which the promise for the Church will be more fully realized. The Church needs in a much stronger degree the powers and the gifts of the Holy Spirit operating in the battle against the satanic powers, against the Antichrist himself. That is why there is given a special promise of the Holy Spirit for the end-time. In the prophecies of the Old Testament, the coming of the Holy Spirit on earth and for the people of Israel was a special sign of the end-time. Of this time it is written: 'Until the Spirit be poured upon us from on high . . .' (Isa. 32:15). 'And it shall come to pass afterward, that I will pour out my spirit upon all flesh' (Joel 2:28). We cannot comprehend how the Holy Spirit works and acts. He even gives gifts to people who have only just accepted Jesus as their Savior. He continues to work in their hearts and He sees to it that these gifts will be used in the right way by bringing them into a healthy inward attitude, step by step, until the image of Jesus Christ is formed in us. He equips us with gifts and power. He also sees to it, as we read in the Book of Acts, that we humble ourselves over and over again and fight against sin. He creates burning desire within us, to follow after *agape* love more and more, and to achieve the full power of Jesus Christ through this inner attitude of the Spirit, in love. All this we owe to the Holy Spirit, who in His grace grants us these gifts; who leads us, admonishes us and convinces us; who wages war in us against the flesh; who prays and pleads. He is the life-giving Spirit, who renews us and fills our lives with prayer, and with fire to be His witnesses and to confess Jesus Christ.

The Gifts of the Holy Spirit in This Time

"In the Acts of the Apostles we see that the kingdom of God, the Church of Jesus Christ, was built through the work of the Holy Spirit, His fruit and His gifts. The Word of God shows us that there is no substitute for the gifts of the Spirit. They were not only for that time, but also for today. The good Shepherd will give to His own a life which

reveals His Spirit and power. For this equipment is necessary for the life of the Church,
in her battle against the powers of darkness
now, as in those days. Through the gifts, the
Head of the Body gives power to its members, to resist deceiving spirits in every form.
Also at this time, He gives her the gift of discernment of spirits, when new and deceiving powers are threatening the Church. He
also gives her the gift of faith and of the
working of miracles, when we stand today
threatened by nuclear war. When the evidence of the unfolding of the power of the
Antichrist becomes visible, then the Lord
gives to His Church, through the gift of wisdom, the right word for this situation. The
first Christian church, which was brought
to life in an unusual way through the cre-
ating power of the Holy Spirit, needed the
gifts of the Spirit to be built up. How much
more do we need the gifts of the Spirit in
this time in our churches and groups, where
life is so often absent! One appeals to tra-
dition and habits and refuses to acknowledge the truth which the Bible teaches us:
'The letter killeth, but the spirit giveth life'
(2 Cor. 3:6). But this Spirit does not reveal
Himself apart from the gifts of grace. The
'letter', as the apostle writes, that is to say,

pious human effort to understand and grasp the Word of God, cannot be a substitute for these. Only the Spirit can give light. Only He can touch the heart. Only He can lead us to repentance, humility and reconciliation. The Spirit alone makes us understand the signs of the times and He shows us that we have to stand in the gap for a world that is doomed to destruction.

"Only the life-giving Spirit who gives His gifts can prepare the Church for the coming of the Lord. Real church life, as we see it in the Book of Acts, is inconceivable without the work of the Holy Spirit and His gifts. For the believers in the first church this was self-evident, because they had all received the Holy Spirit. And why should it be any different today? The New Testament considers the functioning of the gifts of the Spirit as an organic result and a self-evident phenomenon accompanying the receiving and working of the Holy Spirit. In the Bible you cannot find one single place that gives us any indication that the gifts of the Spirit were only necessary for the apostolic times. The slow 'drying up' of the stream of the gifts of the Spirit in the post-apostolic period (there has always been a little trickle) is not in accordance with the Biblical and histor-

ical plan of God's salvation. We must seek
the reason for this in lack of faith and in the
backsliding of the Church. Lack of alert-
ness, obedience and faith can make it impossible for Christ to speak as intimately and
as wonderfully as 'in the days of her youth'
(Hosea 2:15).

"The gifts of the Spirit have a function
which cannot be replaced by anything else.
The gifts are a sign of a further penetrating
work of Christ, out of the matchlessness of
eternity into this poor world. Since the tri-
une God has been declared dead by some,
we need evidence that He lives! People must
be confronted today with the reality of the
Holy Spirit, who in truth glorifies the Father
and the Son, when He gives people His gifts,
such as the gifts of faith, of working miracles and of healing, in love; for through these
the greatness and the omnipotence of God
shines as a light. Testimonies of the life of
the Holy Spirit in the Church of Jesus Christ
are very necessary today. Therefore we need
men and women who are full of the Spirit,
in whom the gifts of grace are active. Such
people can show the world that God is alive.
Also through the gifts of healing, Jesus glorifies Himself today. Jesus once performed
miracles of healing to show that the power

and the works of the devil are destroyed, and that His kingdom is coming: 'He went about doing good and healing all who suffered from the devil's power—because God was with him' (Acts 10:38 PHILLIPS).

"This gift of healing is promised to all who believe in Him (Mark 16:18), and particularly to the elders. We must always be prepared to lay on hands (James 5:14), because as a matter of fact every sick person in the church has to be brought first to Jesus, for He says: 'Come unto me, all ye that labor and are heavy laden.'

"So we must measure the value of the gifts in accordance with what is written in Holy Scripture, where they are shown to be important. We must not measure their value incorrectly, or underestimate their importance, because in some cases they have been misused. There have also been false prophets, and sometimes there has been the misuse of the gifts of healing and of tongues. To question or deny their value would be denying the evidence of the Bible. When the Holy Scripture says: 'Desire spiritual gifts' (1 Cor. 14:1), then we cannot substitute for it 'Keep away from the gifts of the Spirit,' or 'Fight against them,' simply because there have been false prophets and prophecies which have possibly been straight from the devil. We can only fight against the misuse, never against the gifts themselves.

"What a responsibility! God offers to His Church these gifts, but on condition that we must pray for them. Very often we do not do that, and therefore we are so poor and in want. So we become guilty of the lives of many people who perhaps could have found the way to Jesus, if the gifts had been active. For God uses not only the preaching of the Word, but He also uses today all the gifts which the Word of God promises us, so that He will be glorified by them, the Church built up, and those who stand far off come to believe in Him. This also applies to the gift of speaking in tongues. Should the Holy Spirit, who is still the same, suddenly let one of His gifts of grace disappear, when Jesus Himself mentioned it as one of the signs that should follow believers? It is just this gift, which gives us words to worship Him, when the words of our human language are not sufficient, because the glory and the love of God are so great, that our mother tongue does not have the words to express it. But the Holy Spirit Himself 'maketh intercession for us with groanings which cannot be uttered' (Rom. 8:26). He, who is the only

One who can fathom the depths of God, gives us words of adoration of the all-mighty, holy, eternal God, whose Being we can never understand. We praise Him in these new tongues, languages which are given through the Spirit."

Thus Mother Basilea has spoken. And what joy that the Holy Spirit gives us even God's own love in our hearts (Rom. 5:5), for gifts without love are nothing.

> If I speak with the eloquence of men and of angels, but have no love, I become no more than blaring brass or crashing cymbal. If I have the gift of foretelling the future and hold in my mind not only all human knowledge but the very secrets of God, and if I also have that absolute faith which can move mountains, but have no love, I amount to nothing at all. If I dispose of all that I possess, yes, even if I give my own body to be burned, but have no love, I achieve precisely nothing.
>
> 1 Corinthians 13:1–3 PHILLIPS

10
Victory through Yielding

Are you prepared for the coming of Jesus? Am I prepared for the coming of Jesus? It is so wonderful that it is written so clearly in the Bible—it is only by full surrender that we are made ready for His coming again. If it depended on us, then one day we would be successful, but the next day just the opposite. William Nagenda, an evangelist from Uganda, has given us a very good example of what surrender means. He told that one day he arrived home after a long trip. There his little son of three stood at the station waiting for him.

"Daddy, I will carry your suitcase," he said.

William did not want to disappoint him and said: "All right, put your hand on my hand."

So they went on their way and the little boy kept his weak little hand on the strong hand of his father. They came home and the little boy said: "Mummy, I carried Daddy's suitcase."

So it is with us. Our hands are not strong enough, but when we lay our weak hand on the strong hand of Jesus, then He Himself prepares us for His coming again. We must not forget "that the One who has begun his good work in you will go on developing it until the day of Jesus Christ" (Phil. 1:6 PHILLIPS).

We shall not be so ignorant as the little boy and say: "I carried the suitcase!" We shall honor the Lord for all this. We shall see Jesus face to face, and it is important whether we shall see Him as our Judge or as our Redeemer. Have you put your weak hand on the strong hand of your Savior? Do you believe that Jesus can help you? Paul says: "For I know the one in whom I have placed my confidence, and I am perfectly certain that the work he has committed to me is safe in his hands until that day" (2 Tim. 1:12 PHILLIPS).

There is still a tremendous struggle and fight, but the moment comes when our sanctification is complete. In 1 Thessalonians 3:12–13 it is written that this will really happen: "May the Lord give you the same increasing and overflowing love for each other and toward all men as we have toward you. May he establish you, holy and blameless in heart and soul, before himself, the Father of us all" (PHILLIPS). Yes, the best is yet to be! One day there will be an end to the battle. Then there will be the victory, victory through Jesus Christ! "May the God of peace make you holy through and through. May you be kept in soul and mind and body in spotless integrity until the coming of our Lord Jesus Christ" (1 Thess. 5:23 PHILLIPS).

Full surrender includes also our mistakes and errors. Once, somebody visited a weavers' school. He asked one of the pupils: "What do you do when you have made a mistake? Can you cut it out, or must you start again from the very beginning?"

The pupil said: "No, our teacher is such a great artist that when we make a mistake, he uses that to increase the beauty of the pattern."

That is what Jesus does with us! Our feeling of inferiority is really pride, because we will not accept that our ability is limited. We want to be better than we really are.

But it is so wonderful that when we acknowledge our mistakes, the Lord sometimes uses them to His honor. I remember that when I was in Japan the first time, I had the problem that to me most Japanese looked alike. That lasted about a month. One finds that when a Japanese comes to our country, he thinks the same. But I found it difficult. Once I had to lead a Bible study group for students. During the meeting I saw someone entering the room. I thought: "Oh, that is the director of the Bible school!" But he was not; he was a professor of a non-Christian university. When I had finished my talk I asked this man: "Will you close this meeting with prayer?"

The professor was startled: "I have never prayed before."

Then I saw my mistake. I recognized him and said: "Oh, that does not matter; I will do it, Professor."

But Japanese people are very polite and after the meeting he came to me, bowed very deeply, and said: "I am so sorry that I could not comply with your request, but I do not know how to pray."

"I have a great deal of respect for you, Professor, because you have not done it. If you had been a superficial man, then perhaps you might have said a prayer without believing it. It was very good that you did not do it." Then I asked: "But why are you not a Christian?"

"Then I should first have to study Christianity."

"It is not written in my Bible: 'To him who studies Christianity God gives power to become a child of God,' but rather 'As many as received him, to them gave he the power to become the sons of God' (John 1:12)."

Then I started to show him the way of salvation. But while I preached the gospel to him, I prayed quietly in my heart. Someone who is counseling must always have at the same moment the horizontal and the vertical connections at work. After half an hour this professor came to the decision that made the angels in heaven rejoice, the decision for Jesus! Here you see how the Lord used the mistake of foolish Corrie ten Boom to give this man the opportunity to be saved for eternity. This professor had a strategically important position in the University of Tokyo. Of course, we cannot make a system of this. Not everyone who goes to India discovers America! But by all means we must lay our failures in the hands of the Lord. When there is total surrender, then we walk relaxed at the hand of the Savior.

PART 3

Equipment for Active Service

11
Love

~~~

When I was in a concentration camp during the last war, we had to stand every day for two or three hours for roll call, often in the icy cold wind. That was something terrible. Once a woman guard used these hours to demonstrate her cruelty. I could hardly bear to see and hear what happened in front of me. Suddenly a skylark started to sing high in the sky. We all looked up, and when I looked to the sky and listened to its song, I looked still higher and thought of Psalm 103:11: "For as the heavens are high above the earth, so great is his steadfast love toward those who fear him" (RSV). Suddenly I saw that this love of God was a greater reality than the cruelty that I experienced myself and saw around me. "Oh, the love of God, how deep and great, far deeper than man's deepest hate." God sent that skylark every day for three weeks, just at the time of roll call, to give us an opportunity to turn away our eyes from the cruelty of men to the ocean of God's love. This love is a protection as well as a weapon. It guards us against impatience, against zeal without sense, against annoyance, against bitterness, against gloating. It is a very strong weapon in the battle to win souls, for it never gives in. It is slow to lose patience, it looks for a way of being constructive, it is glad with all good men when truth prevails. Love knows no limit to its endurance, no end to its trust, no fading of its hope; it can outlast anything. It is, in fact, the one thing that still stands when all else has fallen (1 Corinthians 13).

How do we get that strong love? It is the Holy Spirit who gives us that love (Rom. 5:5).

The First Love

When I had been wandering around the world as a "tramp for the Lord" for twenty years, I suddenly fell ill. The doctor said to me: "If you continue with this work, then you will stand it only for one more year; but if you go on furlough for a year, then you can perhaps work for another ten years." I consulted my "Employer," my Savior, and He said very clearly that this advice of the doctor was in His plan. I could live during that "Sabbath year" in Lweza, a beautiful house in Uganda. It is a house with a nice park around it. The climate is ideal. Nature is so matchless. There one has a view from the garden over Lake Victoria. I could work there a little bit. There are many universities, churches, prisons, and groups in Kampala, the nearby town. So, with two or three meetings every week, my spirit remained active. But sleeping every night in the same bed gave me a great rest during that time. During these last twenty years I have slept perhaps in more than a thousand different beds.

In November the "Sabbath year" had gone by. Conny, my fellow worker, and I put the world map on my bed to make plans for a whole year. Our method is always the same; first we listen to what God's plan is and then we sign it. We will be "planned" by Him. It became a very good program: three months in different countries in Africa, two months in America, three months in Eastern Europe behind the Iron Curtain. But my heart did not rejoice. When I was alone I said to the Lord: "I prefer to stay here. There is so much to do in Kampala and Entebbe, the two nearest cities. I will work for You, I am willing to have meetings every day, pastoral care, writing books, but please, let me sleep every night in the same bed. Everyone can understand that I, at my age, should take it a bit easier." I was then seventy-three. This new plan of mine made me really happy.

Then Conny called me; there was a visitor. It was an African minister from Ruanda. He started immediately to welcome me: "We are so glad that you are willing to come to Ruanda again. Five years ago you helped us so marvelously when you told what the Lord had been to you in your great need. You said at that time: 'It was not my faith that helped me through three prisons. My faith was weak and was often wavering. It was the Lord Himself who carried me through. He promised: "I am with you all the days." I have always believed, but now I know from experience that Jesus' light is stronger than the deepest darkness. It is good that I can tell you that. If you should meet great difficulties, then you could say: "I have not Corrie ten Boom's faith," but when it is Jesus, then you can trust that the same Savior who helped Corrie ten Boom will also carry you through.'"

The African brother continued: "That was all very interesting to me, but I had never been in prison. For many of us it was just a bit of theory, but in these five years there has been civil war in our country. Many of us have been in prison. I myself was for two years in a cell. Then we remembered everything you had said and it was a great comfort to us. That is why we are so happy that you are now coming again to Ruanda."

But I was not happy at all. His words were different from what I wanted. It is always good in such a situation to ask a question yourself. Then you can lead the conversation in another direction. That is why I asked: "How is the church in Ruanda? What kind of message do they need now?" Without hesitating one moment the brother opened his Bible and read:

Write this to the angel of the Church in Ephesus:

These words are spoken by the one who holds the seven stars safe in his right hand, and who walks among the seven golden lampstands. I know what you have done; I know how hard you have worked and what you have endured. I know that you will not tolerate wicked men, that you have put to the test self-styled "apostles," who are nothing of the sort, and have found them to be liars. I know your powers of endurance—how you have suffered for the sake of my name and have not grown weary. But I hold this against you, that you do not love as you did at first. Remember then how far you have fallen. Repent and live as you lived at first. Otherwise, if your heart remains unchanged, I shall come to you and remove your lampstand from its place.

Revelation 2:1–6 PHILLIPS

This arrow penetrated my heart. Not only Ruanda, not only the church of Ephesus, but also Corrie ten Boom needed this message! I had lost my first love. Twenty years before I had come out of a concentration camp, starved, weak, but in my heart there was a burning love; love for the Lord, who had carried me through so faithfully; love for the people around me, a longing to tell them—Jesus is a reality, He lives, He is Victor, I know it from experience! I went to Germany and lived in the midst of ruins. I was interested in winning souls for eternity, to glorify the Lord, so that everyone should hear: We can never fall so deeply, always deeper are the everlasting arms that carry us.

Yes, that was at that time, and now? Now I was interested in my bed. I had lost my first love. Then I read Revelation 2:5, ". . . except thou repent." Suddenly joy came in my heart. I saw that the door to repentance was wide open! I could bring my sin, my cold heart, to Him who is faithful and just (1 John 1:7, 9). I did it; I confessed my sins and asked for forgiveness. And then happened what always happens when we bring a sin to God in the name of Jesus: He forgave me. Jesus cleansed my heart with His blood, and a heart which is cleansed by the blood of Jesus, He fills with the Holy Spirit. The fruit of the Spirit is love! Not my first love, but a much greater love; God's love was poured out into my heart. I went again on my journeys. What a great joy it was to experience the love of God, who gave me rivers of living water for the thirsty world of Africa, America, and Eastern Europe. Of course, it can be the will of God that old people retire from their work, and in great thankfulness to the Lord enjoy their pensions, but for me the way of obedience is to travel on, although not as much as before.

The doctor has allowed me to work for seventy percent of the time. In this time we must be vigilant. Jesus has warned us in Matthew 24:12 that the love of most men waxes cold, because iniquity abounds. It is very easy to belong to the "most men," but the gate of conversion is wide open. Hallelujah!

Love for the Enemy

When Jesus tells us to love our enemies, He Himself gives us the love that He demands from us.

In Africa I visited the cell of a young man who was sentenced to death. His hands were chained and his dark skin had many red wounds, caused by lashes. Behind me stood three soldiers. The cell was absolutely empty; only a plank on the floor and high up in the wall a very little window. The prisoner looked very healthy and strong. The tragedy that this man had to die overwhelmed me.

I sat down beside him and prayed for a word from the Lord. "Have you ever heard of the cross of Jesus Christ, where He carried the sins of the whole world, also your sins?" He nodded. "Do you believe in Jesus Christ, that He will be your Savior too?"

"Yes, I love Him, but I have not always been faithful. Politics have taken up my time and attention completely, but now I have brought all my sins to Jesus. He has forgiven me. If I may live any longer, then I will serve Him with all my life."

"Have you forgiven the people that have brought you here, who have your death on their conscience?"

"No, I hate them."

"I can understand that. I will tell you one of my experiences. During the war in Holland, I helped to save Jewish people, because Hitler wanted to kill them. One day a man came to me who told me that his wife had also helped the Jews and that now she had been arrested. 'She is in the police station and probably she will be put to death. Now there is a policeman who is willing to let her escape, if we pay him six hundred guilders, but I have no money,' he told me. 'I can help you,' I said. 'Come back in an hour.' In the meantime I collected all the money from my friends and all I had myself, and it was exactly six hundred guilders. I gave it to him to save the life of his wife. But he was a betrayer. His wife was not arrested at all. The enemy had told him to find out whether I helped Jewish people. So this man thought that at the same time he could make some money out of this situation. He went home with six hundred guilders in his pocket. But five minutes later the enemy came and my whole family was arrested. Later, when I heard that this man had betrayed us, hatred came into my heart, just as it happened with you. I had given him the last money that I had. But then

I read in the Bible that hatred is really murder in God's eyes (Matt. 5:21–22).

"How glad I was that I knew what I could do against hatred. 'The blood of Jesus Christ His Son cleanseth us from all sin. . . . If we confess our sins, he is faithful and just to forgive us our sins, and to cleanse us from all unrighteousness' (1 John 1:7, 9). I brought my hatred to Jesus. He forgave me and cleansed my heart with His blood. After the war this betrayer was sentenced to death. I wrote to him: 'What you have done through your betrayal caused the death of my eighty-four-year-old father, my brother, his son, and my sister in prison. I myself have terribly suffered through your fault, but I have forgiven you everything. This is just a very little example of the forgiveness and love of Jesus. He lives in my heart; that is why I can forgive you. Jesus will also come into your heart and will make you a child of God. Confess your sins to Him. On the cross of Calvary He has finished all for your sins and mine.' Later he wrote me: 'I have prayed: "Jesus, when You can give such a love for the enemy in the heart of someone who follows You, then there is hope for me." I have indeed confessed my sins to Him. Now I know that I am a child of God, cleansed by the blood of Jesus.'

"So you see that Jesus used me to save the soul of this same man I had hated so much. Do you know that if you do not forgive, you yourself do not receive forgiveness? Jesus said: 'For if you forgive other people their failures, your Heavenly Father will also forgive you. But if you will not forgive other people, neither will your Heavenly Father forgive you your failures' (Matt. 6:14–16 PHILLIPS). You cannot do that, neither can I, but Jesus can!" The same day the prisoner sent a message to his wife: "Forgive my murderers. You are not able to do it, I am not able, but Jesus is able. If we are not willing, then we ourselves do not receive forgiveness."

When Jesus comes and we have bitterness, yes, even hatred in our hearts, then we are not ready to meet Him with a clean heart: "Everyone who has at heart a hope like that keeps himself pure, for he knows how pure Christ is" (1 John 3:3 PHILLIPS).

In the time of the final battle, many will be filled with hatred. If we are not cleansed from bitterness, then we do not stand on victory ground. It is very easy to belong to the masses of people. It is one of the laws of the kingdom of God that men receive peace only if they are always ready to forgive unreservedly. We never touch the love of God so much as when we love our enemies. "The love of God is shed abroad in our hearts by the Holy Ghost which is given unto us" (Rom. 5:5). He does the job. Hallelujah!

12
Fellowship of the Saints

~~~~

"Make sure that your everyday life is worthy of the Gospel of Christ. So that . . . I may know that you are standing fast in a united spirit, battling with a single mind for the faith of the Gospel" (Phil. 1:27 PHILLIPS). When there is no unity in an army, one cannot expect victory. We need the fellowship of the saints. The fruit of the Spirit of Galatians 5:22 makes the fellowship of the children of God a joyful possibility. In this battle it is very essential that we are one in spirit with the other soldiers in the army of Jesus Christ.

We do not need to agree with each other about all doctrines, but through the gift of discernment of the spirits we can find out with whom we can be united in the battle and with whom we cannot. I believe that the Lord is willing to give at this time the discernment of the spirits to his children,

because it is a necessary part of our armor.
We *must* be able to discern the spirits. That
is why the Holy Spirit equips us with this
power. The Bible tells us that in this time
many will try to deceive us, yes, if it were
possible, even the very elect (Matt. 24:24).

I am so glad that there is written: "If it
were possible." Yes, the Lord protects us
from the great danger of being deceived. It
is the Holy Spirit who gives us the love and
the wisdom to have discernment of the spirits instead of criticism. Criticism is a great
danger in our country. Loveless criticism by
a believer nearly ruins the other believer
being criticized. But on the other hand, we
must clearly discern what is from the devil
and what is from the Holy Spirit. We have
to exercise ourselves. The devil is not always
a roaring lion; he can also be very "pious,"
and then it is difficult to discern. But it is
such a joy that we have a "blank check." In
James 1:5 is written: "And if, in the process,
any of you does not know how to meet any
particular problem he has only to ask God—
who gives generously to all men without
making them feel foolish or guilty—and he
may be quite sure that the necessary wisdom will be given him" (PHILLIPS). He gives
it. So we can go through life as wise people,

because His wisdom gives us open ears and eyes.

By the fruit we know the tree. If there is confusion and lovelessness and a spirit of criticism, then we know that the enemy has been busy. But if there is love, if there is a longing to save souls, if there is spiritual activity and joy in prayer and Bible reading, then we know that the Holy Spirit has been at work. "If we really are living in the same light in which he eternally exists, then we have true fellowship with each other" (1 John 1:7 PHILLIPS).

As soon as we come in contact with other people, we detect the weak points of ourselves and of the others, and then it is such a joy that at the end of this text is written: "The blood which He shed for us keeps us clean from any and every sin." The finished work at the cross is our salvation. When Jesus died there, He carried the sins of the whole world. That is why we can bring our sins directly to Him and He cleanses us. When the blood of Jesus cleanses us, He does it completely. We can walk in light because He is in the light, and not because we have the light in ourselves.

You and I can walk in the light because Jesus lives, because Jesus is Victor, and because we can expect all from Him. We are like the moon, not like the sun. The sun has light from itself, the moon only reflects the light. God educates us through our fellowship with others.

Sometimes we need a little grindstone to polish our character. By nature my heart is proud. Besides this, all over the world so much love is shown to me and I am held in high esteem by so many everywhere, that there is a great danger of becoming "somebody." Then I must decrease, and therefore the Lord uses fellow Christians. I had started a work for which I had a great love in my heart, but my friends, who in fact carried out this work for me because I was always traveling, could not agree with the aim and with my way of bringing the gospel. Then they asked me to withdraw and to give them free hand. I became angry and bitterness came into my heart. I confessed it immediately to the Lord and He took it away; I could forgive my friends. But during the night I awoke and my first thought was how had it been possible that my friends had been so unkind, had behaved almost like enemies. Then I saw that in fact my heart was not yet free. Again I immediately confessed it to the Lord. I thought

I had the victory, but the next night it came again. Is this because one does not carry the armor of God consciously during the night? Does the enemy know that when we are asleep we are not ready for battle? It is necessary that in the evening before we go to sleep our whole being and also our subconsciousness is cleansed and that we fully surrender to Him so that there is not a single starting point left for the enemy.

I complained about it to the Lord: "Why am I still so angry? I have experienced that You gave me grace to forgive even those who murdered my family during the war. I have always been able to preach to other people that when You tell us to love our enemies, You give us the love that You require from us. Why is there still bitterness in my heart? Lord, when I remember how often You have forgiven me in more than seventy years of life, why is it difficult for me to forgive this? Lord, this is a problem, for I know that if I do not forgive, You will not forgive me." Then I became quiet.

That same day I heard a good illustration. When someone has been ringing the church bells—bim-bam, bim-bam—there comes the moment when he stops, no matter whether it is done electrically or by hand.

But after that there often comes another bim-bam, then again a bim, then again a bam, and perhaps still a few times more. But he does not worry about that, because he knows that there has come an end to the bell-ringing, and very soon the bim-bams will stop. So it is also with the bitterness one has brought to the Lord. Bim-bams can come back, but then we must simply bring them again to the Lord. He is Victor, and soon He makes it possible by the Holy Spirit that instead of being annoyed, we love those who have sinned against us. When other people make it hard for us, then we must pray that the Lord will use this for our sanctification. Pray for them and love them as the Holy Spirit in us loves them. Then this becomes a practical training for the victory of the final battle. This experience has helped me to counsel many other people who had to resist the same temptations. I was not able to do it, but Jesus was Victor. He gave it to me. That helped them to turn their eyes in the right direction to look on high. I have learned still more. I have seen that my heart was too much tied to this work. I would not give in because my sister Betsie had inspired me to start it, for what God had told her at that time in the concentration camp had become my mission later on.

So I had to learn not to live out of the past, but to be obedient to the vocation I had to fulfill now. The Lord also sets us free from the bonds of the good past. If we will follow Jesus in all things, then we go the way of the cross and this includes too that very often we are not understood even by our own friends. The Lord gives grace to be able to accept fully this being misunderstood. When I get bitter feelings against my friends, then I pray to the Lord Jesus to take up my thoughts. In my imagination I have a talk with Him and my friends together. Then He gives His love and peace, and all bitterness disappears out of my heart. This experience has made me richer and stronger.

When Jesus was arrested there were three reactions among the disciples. Peter struck out and the ear of Malchus was cut off; several disciples ran away; John remained behind with Jesus and suffered with Him. Cross-bearing means to suffer with Jesus. So we may fill up in our daily lives "that which is behind of the afflictions of Christ in [our] flesh" (Col. 1:24). It is not my job to persuade my friends, only the Holy Spirit convicts of sins. We have only to deal with our own sins and we must pray: "Search me, O God, and know my heart: try me, and know my thoughts: and see if there be any wicked way in me, and lead me in the way everlasting" (Ps. 139:23–24).

13

Devotion in Service

The time of training is a time of active service. When we know that we are in an important battle and also know that this battle will be victorious, then there is a radiance on all our daily adventures. These experiences need not be extraordinary, but one sees all kinds of work as a part of the victory and the building of the kingdom of God.

My father often said: "My name is on the shop, but it would be proper to have God's name on the window. I am a watchmaker by the grace of God. It is God's watchmaker's shop." When we start to see more or less everything from God's point of view, then we always seek and find opportunities to help others.

In Brazil lives a very simple woman. She loves the Lord. Her friends went every week to a women's prison to take the gospel through preaching, singing, and counseling. She could not take part in this for she could not do such things, but she had love in her heart! One thing she knew very well—baking cakes. She suggested to her friends that she go with them and take a cake with her. I got an invitation to speak there and I will never forget it. All the women in this prison came. The beginning was not pleasant. We were searched by the guards, our bags were opened, they fingered our clothes in case we had hidden something. But after that the women who had come with me started to sing hymns and I brought the Word. Then, when we were through with everything the moment came that seemed to be the climax for the prisoners.

Our friend brought in the cake she had made. She had taken a knife with her and cut the cake in many little pieces. Then she had also brought along little pieces of paper in many different colors. Every piece of cake was nicely packed and offered to the women. In the love of her heart she had understood what colors mean for prisoners. It was a feast, a real feast; everyone was happy. People laughed, everyone was kind to one another and when we went, we left these women with a blessing in their hearts. Poor stranded lives, murderesses and thieves, but they had heard the Word of God and they had experienced the love of God through the kindness of this simple woman! Every week she does that and the women know and count on it, that after the preaching of the gospel this little treat comes too. Yes, everyone can work in this training time. This simple, faithful woman will one day hear: "I was in prison and you came to Me and gave Me cake."

Chain Reactions

In Australia I was at a very big meeting and at the end I invited the people who wanted to be saved to come forward. The first who came were two little girls. I had told the people that they could go to a room behind the altar, but these children had not understood that. They stopped in front of me, and one asked with a very clear little voice, so that everyone in the church heard: "Am I too small to ask Jesus to come into my heart?"

"No, not at all. Jesus was interested even in sparrows and you are much bigger than a sparrow! Jesus said: 'Let the little children come unto me!' I myself was five years old when I asked Jesus to come into my heart and He came in and He has never left me."

Then the little girl said aloud, so that the whole church could hear it: "Lord Jesus, I have been very naughty. Will You come into my heart and cleanse it with Your blood?" And Jesus came in.

That is what He said in Revelation 3:20: "Behold, I stand at the door, and knock: if any man hear my voice, and open the door, I will come in to him." And it is just as certain that He will come in, when you, who read this, open your heart's door to Him. He does not ask: "What is your age?"

I said to the other girl: "Will you do the same?"

Then the little one said: "I did it three weeks ago, and after that I prayed every day for Betty, and now Betty has done it!"

"Then you must pray together for a third girl."

They looked at each other very thoughtfully and said at the same moment: "Anne. That must be Anne!" And then they promised to pray for Anne, until the Lord would knock at her heart and when Anne had opened her heart for Jesus, they would pray together with Anne for a fourth girl and so on.

This is the chain reaction of the gospel which started in the hearts of two little girls, who were perhaps not yet eight years old. This chain reaction of intercession can start in everyone's heart, and so everyone can cooperate to prepare the coming of the Lord Jesus, now today!

Then there was the youth group in Invercargill to which I spoke. It was a tremendously blessed evening; the Holy Spirit worked in hearts. There were about thirty young people. A year later I came back. I met the minister and asked how his youth group was going on.

"Oh," he said, "it goes very well. Will you please speak to them again? They meet tonight."

I went, but when I entered the hall, I said: "I will be very happy to bring a message here, but I had meant a different group. There are about two hundred young people here. I meant that group of thirty, but it does not matter at all."

"But this *is* the same group," they said. "When the Holy Spirit began to work in our hearts, we got a real longing to win souls. One evening a week we came together for Bible study and intercession. Everyone could mention a name of a friend or someone who did not know the Lord yet. But then they had to speak to them about the Lord Jesus in the course of that same week. When that other person came to know the Lord, then he or she was invited to come also. But this person had sometimes three or four other people to pray for, and so it worked like a snowball that became bigger and bigger. Now there are more than two hundred. Several of them have gone to Bible school!"

What God can do with the life of one person who understands that he is a little part of the kingdom of God, at a time in which we can expect that Jesus comes soon! God has a plan. The "fullness of the Gentiles" must come. And when the last of them comes to faith, then it is the fullness of time. Everyone who is used by the Lord to bring other people to Him cooperates to prepare the second coming of the Lord and to hasten it.

14
Faithfulness

—————— ∞∞∞∞ ——————

"When thou vowest a vow unto God, defer not to pay it; for he hath no pleasure in fools" (Eccl. 5:4). To be a conqueror it is very important to remain faithful. It is good to ask yourself: "Did I ever vow to God, and then not keep it?" Have you ever been singing with your whole heart after an inspiring talk: "Take my life and let it be consecrated, Lord, to Thee. Take my silver and my gold; take my moments and my days . . ."?

Have you ever said to the Lord: "I will go to the place where you send me, even to the mission field"? Did you then go to your work again without paying any attention to the marching orders of the Master? Did you then allow that promise just to disappear out of your heart?

Have you ever promised to give your tithes to the Lord? Did you ever tell Him that you would never speak negatively about other people and never exaggerate? Have you ever said any of these things to the Lord and not done them? Then you are not faithful.

In Revelation 2:10 is written: "Be faithful unto death, and I will give you the crown of life" (RSV).

In Judges 6 the story of Gideon begins. He was really very small even in his own eyes, but he received a mission from God and he did not dare do it. In verse 13 we read that there was rebellion in his heart. He complained and was without courage. He did not go at all. Then God said to him: "Go in this thy might." Gideon had feelings of inferiority. He made excuses. "My family is poor in Manasseh, and I am the least in my father's house."

Did you know that feeling inferior is pride, and that you are not willing to accept your limitations? God's answer was: "I am with you." Gideon had very little faith and said: "Show me a sign." He received it. Gideon was afraid and the Lord said: "Peace be unto you."

In Revelation 21 the fearful people are mentioned together with unbelievers, murderers, whoremongers, idolaters, etc. Cowardice is a sin that deserves judgment. When we continue to read the story of Gideon, we see that this little man destroyed the idol of his father, a very dangerous thing to do, as his fellow townsmen could kill him for it. Then God commanded him to attack the enemy and his faith was tried. "But the spirit of the LORD came upon Gideon, and he blew a trumpet" (Judg. 6:34). Gideon obeyed, and finally he overcame a whole army with a gang of three hundred men. How did that happen? Gideon had not a great faith, but he had faith in a great God.

The fruit of the Spirit is faithfulness. And for those who are in training for the final battle, the encouragement stands that God's faithfulness is for us. "Great is thy faithfulness" (Lam. 3:23).

Our faithfulness to God is the fruit of the Spirit. That becomes a quality in us only when we give room to the Holy Spirit in our hearts and lives. Be filled with God's Spirit, and faithfulness, the fruit of the Spirit, will be your portion.

God said to Gideon: "Go in this thy might." It is wonderful that God gives us His strength and that God's strength is demonstrated in our weakness.

I was in Argentina. One day I was asked to visit some patients in a hospital. There had been a terrible polio epidemic. For the first time in my life I saw people lying in iron lungs. The tragedy so overcame me that I could hardly bear it. A nurse asked me: "Will you speak with that Jewish man there?" He was not in an iron lung, but lay on a bed that went up and down. When his legs went up, his midriff pushed against his lungs and he could breath out. When his legs went down, he could breathe in. He was fed by a little tube in his nose. He could not speak but he could write. When I looked at him I said in despair: "Oh, Lord, I cannot do this. Please let me go somewhere else, so that I can cry in a little corner. I am not able to speak to this man." When I say to the Lord: "I cannot do this," I always receive the answer: "I have known that for a long time, but it is good that you know it too, for now you can let Me do it."

And I said: "Now Lord, then you do it." And He did. I could speak to this man. I showed him an embroidery, that on one side shows only a tangle of threads, but on the other a beautiful crown. I said: "When I see you lying on this bed I think of this embroidery. There has been a time in my life when it seemed like the tangled side of this crown. I saw no pattern, no beauty, no harmony. I was in prison, where my sister died before my eyes. But all that time I knew that God has no problems, only plans. There is never panic in heaven. Later on I saw God's side of the pattern. Because I have had to go through deep suffering in that prison, I was able to comfort people afterwards, because I could tell them: Jesus' light is stronger than the deepest darkness. When you have experienced the darkness of a concentration camp, you know how deep that darkness can be!"

Then I spoke to him about the Messiah, Jesus, the Son of God, who died on the cross for our sins. It seemed that when He died the whole plan of His life was broken, but just there He has given the answer to the problem of the sin of the whole world, for He has carried our punishment. And this Jesus did not only *die* for us, but he lives, for He is risen from the dead and He has said: "Lo, I am with you all the days . . . to the [very] close and consummation of the age" (Matt. 28:20 ANT). He will even live in our hearts. We may use His name and pray in His name. And so I told him the happy message of Jesus' death and life. The man took a piece of paper and wrote: "I see already the beautiful side of the embroidery of my life."

What a victory it was for him to lie there, not being able to move, or speak, or breathe, and in spite of all this, to see God's side. That was really a very great miracle. We had a good time together and I was so thankful. I could pray and then thank the Lord with him. The next day I went again to the hospital and asked the nurse: "May I speak with him again?" She told me that he had beckoned her when I had left, and then wrote on his little writing pad: "For the first time in my life I have prayed in Jesus' name." Then he closed his eyes and died. This Jewish man had found Jesus in the last moment of his life. And God had used me for that when I was not able to do it. Yes, God's strength is demonstrated in our weakness.

When the marching orders of our King are given and seem very exacting, then we need not fear, for He Himself gives us the courage, the faithfulness, and the strength to obey Him. "Go in this thy might," He says when He has given us, through the Holy Spirit, the fruit of the Spirit, faithfulness and strength. "If we are faithless He always remains faithful. He cannot deny his own nature" (2 Tim. 2:13 PHILLIPS).

15
Faith

~~~~~~

We are often in danger when we look at our own faith. But in Hebrews 12:2 is written: "Let . . . our eyes [be] fixed on Jesus the source and the goal of our faith" (PHILLIPS). Before the war I had a watchmaker's shop. Sometimes it happened that a new watch I had in the shop did not run well. Then I did not repair it, but sent it back to the factory. When the manufacturer had repaired the watch it went exactly right.

When my faith does not work, when I am too busy with myself, then something is not right. But I do not think about repairing my faith myself. I do the same as I did with the watch. I send it back to the manufacturer. He only, the Lord who made my faith, can renew it. When He has repaired it, then my faith works again. Here again we need to change the direction of our looking, away from our faith, unto Jesus.

Hudson Taylor, a great hero of faith, has said: "We do not need a great faith, but we need faith in a great God." And this we have! The almighty God! Jesus speaks about a faith as small as a mustard seed and yet so dynamic that it can remove mountains. The Pharisees showed their faith; they carried it to the marketplace, to the corners of the street, into the temple, so that everyone could see it, but their faith had no power, it was empty.

As we are ourselves, so our faith also is hidden with Jesus in God. That is what we have to learn. We are like fighters who are sent into the world, as into an arena, to fight in the strength of our faith and to conquer. Perhaps there is no other place where the change of direction of our looking is so necessary than just here. Look away from yourself and your faith; look to Him, the Author and Finisher of our faith. He gives you all the faith you need today. It does not help you to look at the petrol in your tank. Invisible, a source of power, ready for use, the petrol is in the tank. And so it is with faith. It is given to you not to admire, but to experience its working.

Faith works to protect us against the fiery arrows of the enemy.

The Shield of Faith

The enemy shoots his fiery arrows out of invisible, unexpected positions. Therefore, this shield is so important. David said: "The Lord is my . . . shield" (Ps. 28:7). God said to Abraham: "I am thy shield, and thy exceeding great reward" (Gen. 15:1).

Not only is faith our shield; the Lord Himself is our shield also. A soldier who handles a shield does not put it behind him, but in front of him. Then he is covered. That is the right position. When the Lord is our shield, He must go before us, and we must remain behind Him. Many are willing to work for the Lord, but they walk in front of Him, and thus the fiery arrows of the evil one can reach them without difficulty.

No, the Lord says: "Follow Me!" He will go before us. Our position demands that we work only on His instructions and go where He calls us. Sometimes we have to wait until the Lord tells it to us very clearly. If we work out of our own enthusiasm, we can expect defeat. Even a small service must be inspired by the Lord. Our prayer should be: "Lord, what do You want me to do? Where must I go?" We can then remain in the center of the will of God, and there it is safe.

If the direction is not yet quite clear, we must wait on the Lord, and this waiting can be a blessing. When we follow Him, we live in the attitude of faith. It is this attitude of faith that keeps us close to the Lord, to Him who gives us the power of faith. When the enthusiasm comes from ourselves, we can be very active, but without instruction from the Master we go unprotected in front of Him, so that the fiery arrows of the devil can do their horrible work unhindered.

When the Lord tells us: "Do this!" He also gives us the faith to do it, and that is why we can obey. Then we will not be ashamed and miracles will happen in our lives. Then we do not work in our own strength, but in the strength we receive from the Lord.

"It is His business, His honor, the cause for which we stand."

Do not begin a work when you are not quite sure that the Lord has instructed you to do it. When fellow Christians tell you that they have had guidance for you, then you may quietly say: "As long as the Lord has not said it to me personally, I will not do it." Paul is an example for us in this matter. He always let the Holy Spirit guide him. If the Holy Spirit said to him: "Do not go there," then he did not go. He really longed to go to all these heathen places in Asia Minor, but the Spirit did not let him do it (Acts 16:6). But once he received a very clear revelation from the Lord that he had to go to Macedonia, he obeyed, and the result was great blessing and miracles. Paul had the true missionary method: obedience.

With the instruction, the Lord gives grace, strength, faith, and courage to carry out the instructed task.

"Where the Lord guides, He provides."

Likewise, when the Holy Spirit gives us special gifts, we may not use these riches according to our own discretion. Again and again, we must look up in faith unto Jesus and say: "Lord, only behind You!" If at this moment the Lord tells you to lay hands on a blind person, then you may not say: "Yes, Lord, but I do not have the gift of healing." When the Lord calls us, then He gives also the courage of faith and everything that we need to carry out the task. When He sends us, then He gives the strength and the grace to obey. The point is to have the right attitude of faith. In the beginning it may be difficult, but by faith we receive strength to reach our goal. If we should have to work up this faith ourselves, then the whole enterprise would become rather doubtful. Today we may be very strong in faith, and tomorrow this may not be so. Today we may feel fine and healthy; tomorrow we may feel ill and weak. So it is with everything that we have from ourselves. Today we may feel like being able to remove mountains; tomorrow we may be without any courage. But when the Lord gives us His faith, it is "eternity faith" that never wavers. It is grounded on God's Word. All these things we must exercise and learn. "Acquaint now thyself with him, and be at peace" (Job 22:21).

A missionary who worked in a dangerous place was once asked: "Are you never afraid?" His answer was: "Yes, sometimes I am, but the rock on which I stand never shakes." He knew that he worked on the instructions of his Master and that was sufficient. His starting point was not his own faith and strength, but the courage of faith that he received from God.

In Galatians 2:20 Paul says: "Yet not I, but Christ liveth in me: and the life which I now live in the flesh I live by the faith of the Son of God, who loved me, and gave himself for me." Not his own faith, but Jesus' faith was his life.

Even those among us who have a strong faith can waver. For instance, look at the disciples. Often Jesus had to say to them: "You of little faith!" How was it with Peter when he was empowered by the Lord to walk on the water? When he saw the waves he doubted and began to sink. As long as we look unto Jesus, He gives us faith. That is why a soldier must always remain behind the shield of faith. So he gets the vision from a safe hiding place. Then the impossible becomes possible.

16
Joy

〰️

"The joy of the LORD is your strength" (Neh. 8:10). It is so important to know that in the final battle the joy of the Holy Spirit is available for us in all circumstances.

Once a prisoner wrote me a letter. "It is Christmas Eve. I am alone in my cell. There are no Christmas presents for me on the table. There is nothing that reminds me of Christmas. On the empty walls there are no Christmas decorations. But in my heart is Christmas joy, because Jesus lives there, and that is the greatest joy a human being can have. I could not send Corrie ten Boom a present, but I went on my knees and prayed for you for two hours. That was my Christmas present for you and it made my own heart still more joyful."

I remember a dark day in Ravensbrück. Betsie and I talked much with the Lord. Horrible things happened around us. There were days that we said to each other: "More terrible than today it can never be." But the next day was still more terrible. Despair was on all faces, for there was no salt in any of the meals that day. When you are slowly starving, salt is very important. Several women died that day, one of them as a result of a cruel beating. The electric light had failed, and after sunset we were in the deepest darkness. I put my arm around Betsie. She spoke about heaven and told me that shortly before we were arrested she had read about heaven in a booklet by the Sadhu Sundar Singh. We had a talk with the Lord. He spoke and we listened; then He listened while we spoke. Then we went to sleep under the dirty coat that we used as a blanket, and Betsie said: "What a wonderful day we have had. The Lord has shown us so much of Himself."

Joy in a Prison in Africa

When it rains in tropical countries, then it really pours. I visited a prison in Ruanda. It was only a small building, but many prisoners were sitting outside on the ground.

"Where do you sleep at night?" I asked.

"Half of us sleep inside, the others must stay outside, because there are too many prisoners."

Some had a banana leaf, others had a branch or an old newspaper to sit on. The uniforms were grey, and the faces of the Negroes were dark and angry. It was all so sad. Could I bring *here* the gospel, the tidings of great joy? No, I could not, but the Holy Spirit could. I prayed: "Lord, the fruit of the Spirit is joy. Give me an ocean of joy to share with these poor fellows."

He did what I asked. I could almost shout for joy. I told them of a Friend whose name is Jesus, who is good and so full of love, who never leaves you alone, who is strong and has the answer for all the great problems of sin and death. I said: "Perhaps you think, 'That is not for us, our lives are too terrible.' But fellows, I was in a prison where it was worse than here, where ninety-five thousand women were killed or died, including my own sister. There I experienced that Jesus is always with me. He lives in my heart; He has never left me alone."

I felt in my heart a great joy that imparted itself to the men who were sitting in the pouring rain. Then I saw that the joy of the Holy Spirit can be experienced in all circumstances. "This Friend and Savior, Jesus, will live in your hearts. Who will open the door of his heart to Him?" They all, including the guards, put up their hands, and their faces beamed.

Jesus came as a light into the world, so that everyone who believes on Him should not abide in darkness (John 12:46).

When I said good-bye, all the prisoners accompanied me to the car. The guards did not seem to be afraid that someone would run away. They came with us and stood around the car.

"What do they say?" I asked my interpreter. She laughed and said: "Old woman, come back, come back, and tell us more about Jesus."

My interpreter, a missionary, said: "I have been here once, but thought it was so hopeless that I stopped my visits. Now I have seen what the Holy Spirit can do. I will come here every week." She has done so, and the feast is going on!

PART 4

Life in the End-Time

17
Signs of the Times

〜〜〜

"Watch therefore, for ye know neither the day nor the hour" (Matt. 25:13). We live now in those days of which Jesus spoke. People are ready to know all about the weather conditions (e.g., when the sun goes down red, it will be nice weather the next day), but what about the signs of the times?

"Ye hypocrites, ye can discern the face of the sky and of the earth; but how is it that ye do not discern this time?" Jesus says (Luke 12:56).

The end-time has started already. Those who pay attention to the signs of the times will not doubt this at all. If we watch the events in the Middle East, in Israel and the Arab States, then we cannot do anything else but look expectantly for the coming of the Lord. Every day, every hour brings us nearer to His coming. We see many more signs of the times than ever before. We can see them in the newspapers. It is a command of the Lord that we must mind the signs of the times. I believe everything that is written in the Bible about the coming again of Jesus. Everything that was written about the first coming of Jesus happened exactly as foretold, so that which is written about His coming again will happen likewise.

This does not mean that I understand everything, but that is not necessary. For instance, in Ezekiel 38 is written that there will be a mighty army coming on horseback. These days soldiers do not go on horseback; they use tanks and airplanes! But now I read in a newspaper that Russia has bought seventy percent of all the horses of the world for its army. What I do not understand of the Bible, I do not throw away, but hang it on a hook, as it were. Later I read or hear more about it, and then, when I understand it, it is added to my knowledge of God's Word, and I just take it off the hook. So it is with Ezekiel 38. What Jesus Himself said in Matthew 24 and in Luke 21 is happening in our days: wars, rumors of wars, one nation against the other, earthquakes, famines, persecution. All this is happening in a far greater measure than ever before.

The clearest sign is Israel, which has returned to its own land. It has, with its six million people, beaten off the threat of a superior force of forty-five million people in the six-day war in June 1967. Many who were concerned about the "apple of God's eye" saw the baffling reality of a swift victory of Israel as a very clear sign of the times.

We do not know the day, neither the hour, in which Jesus will come again. But neither do we know a day nor an hour in which He could not come. The whole world lives now in this expectation; something must happen by which the great problems will be solved. When we look at world history in the light of the Bible, we can find many clear signs: Luke 21:26: "men fainting with fear and with foreboding of what is coming on the world" (RSV). Everywhere in the world are people who are in great fear of an atomic war, and they are rightly afraid. There will be earthquakes, epidemics, and famines. "And because iniquity shall abound, the love of many shall wax cold" (Matt. 24:12).

"Many shall run to and fro, and knowledge shall be increased" (Dan. 12:4). Just look at the development of space travel!

Mother Basilea Schlink says in her book *The End Is Coming,* "It may be true that this end-time has started, so that on the one side many things begin to be outlined on a larger scale, while on the other hand certain things about which we have been in the dark until now, become more clear, though on a smaller scale. Nevertheless, this does not alter the fact that very many details are still secret to us, and we have to wait for the hour that they will be brought to light."

The only thing we have to do is what the Holy Scriptures teach us. We need to raise our voices like the voice of a trumpet so that as many people as possible will awake—first of all those who belong to the church of Christ. We have to proclaim loudly that the end is near, so that people will be startled out of their everyday rest and security by this godly message, as through the roaring of the lion (Amos 3:8); that they will fear and get ready to meet their God. We urgently need such a "blowing of the trumpet," since the day of the Lord draws near, as the prophet Joel says: "Blow the trumpet in Zion, sanctify a fast, call a solemn assembly" (Joel 2:15). For we need to prepare ourselves for all that soon will come to pass.

When we think of the last great battle, we must realize that not only is the future at stake, but that in this present time we are engaged in a warfare. Already we are standing in the midst of the battle. If we have our eyes and ears open, we see how the enemy is marching on from all sides. We do not have to battle against flesh and blood, but against the rulers of the darkness of this world (Eph. 6:12).

The armor is not only necessary for the battle which we have to fight in the future, but also for this time. The devil is a refined psychologist. He has been studying in practice for over six thousand years how to seduce men. He knows our weak spots. He is just like a good cattle dealer who has to go around a cow only once to see all its weak spots. The devil is not omnipresent, but he has an exceptionally good, active secret service at his disposal in his army of demons.

But praise the Lord! "They that be with us are more than they that be with them" (2 Kings 6:16). The Syrian army that the servant of Elisha saw was a terrible, forbidding reality, but when his eyes were opened, he saw something far more important; the angels, a heavenly host with horses and chariots of fire, that had come to protect Elisha. And when we look at this invisible reality, then we know that we stand on victory ground.

In the concentration camp, where I was so often confronted with death, the Lord often gave me grace to see the whole situation more or less in the light of eternity, and then everything was so simple, so uncomplicated. It was as if I saw myself; I stood there, and there stood the devil. The devil was much, much stronger than I, but Jesus stood at my side, and He is far stronger than the devil. And because I stood at Jesus' side, I was more than conqueror. That is reality.

It is essential that we realize in these days that Jesus is Conqueror! To stand at His side, to follow Him, to be hidden with Him in God; that is the safe position for every soldier of Jesus in this time and in the coming final battle.

18
Guidance

∞∞∞

"Don't let the world around you squeeze you into its own mold, but let God remold your minds from within, so that you may prove in practice that the plan of God for you is good, meets all his demands and moves towards the goal of true maturity" (Rom. 12:2 PHILLIPS). A soldier has to know his marching orders. He must know where he has to go and especially it is so important at this time that we see the leading of the Lord very clearly. People often ask me: "How can I know the will of God? How does the Lord lead His children?"

We often make the words "surrender" and "leading" too complicated. When we discover what causes our view to be so dim, the meaning of these words becomes clear. There can be a fog around us, caused by the temptations of the enemy, but it is also possible that the "window" has become dirty on the inside by our sins. It can also happen that God puts His hand on the window, but especially then He is very close to us. We must get accustomed to and train ourselves to be guided by God.

The Holy Spirit makes us sensitive to His guidance. Often we must wait quietly, but waiting on the Lord can be a blessing in itself. We must learn to make our decisions in the presence of the Lord, when we are conscious of His nearness. Often God leads through the Bible, therefore, we must know the Bible well. The better we know the Bible, the more His Word gives light on our path. The Lord also leads us by our feelings. However, when we rely too much on our feelings, we can become too subjective, but it is not necessary that the leading of the Lord has nothing to do with our feelings. Just imagine someone telling you: "I have been married now for six months, but for some weeks I have not felt that I am married." Then there is something wrong with that marriage.

God also uses our feelings to control our relationships with Himself. The fruit of the Spirit is peace and joy, and that does not go without our feelings. Harmony with God goes together with harmony with Spirit-filled believers. Also in this we can find guidance. When God calls us His children, will He then not guide us safely as our Father? "All who follow the leading of God's Spirit are God's own sons" (Rom. 8:14 PHILLIPS).

These things we cannot understand with our logical thinking. We must not forget that all leading of God belongs to the "foolishness of God," which is the highest wisdom, and can only be understood by faith. "We do, of course, speak 'wisdom' among those who are spiritually mature, but it is not what is called wisdom by this world, not by the powers-that-be, who soon will be only the powers that have been. The wisdom we speak of is that mysterious secret wisdom of God which He planned before the Creation for our glory today" (1 Cor. 2:6–7 PHILLIPS).

God wants to take the lead in our lives. He longs for hidden fellowship with His children. In the Bible we read that this fellowship was broken through the fall, but that it is restored again through Jesus Christ. He wants to teach us so that we get to know Him better. He will conform us to His image, and will reach other people through us. But we can only bring His light to others when we are set apart for Him, sanctified. Sanctification means that God separates in our hearts light from darkness. The Holy Spirit brings us nearer to God and makes us conformable to Christ. He convicts us of sin, but He is also the Comforter and He shows us Jesus. Then the separation between light and darkness comes into being. The devil accuses us to discourage us. Every feeling of guilt in our hearts we must confess immediately to the Lord, so that the vision gets clear again. "If the Son therefore shall make you free, ye shall be free indeed" (John 8:36).

The Holy Spirit makes the Bible a love letter from God to His children. When we do not read the Bible often we get confused ideas about God. It is good to pray first before reading the Bible: "Lord, show me my sins." For the Word of God says: "Your sins have hid his face from you" (Isa. 59:2). When we confess our sins, the Lord forgives and His blood cleanses us (1 John 1:7–9).

It is not sufficient to pray: "Lord, help me not to sin." We must humble ourselves, confess our sins, and ask forgiveness. Then He forgives. Let this be our prayer: "Lord, give me today a clear vision of Your leading through the reading of the Bible. Help me also to tell others about what I read in Your

Word." Then you will experience that what you read can help you, and also others through you.

The devil does his utmost to turn our eyes away from Jesus. He tries to get us so far away that we explain everything by our intellect and argue God's Word. We must never forget that the Bible belongs to the plane of God's foolishness. We can never bring the things of foolishness of God down to the lower level of human wisdom, without losing a blessing. But through the Holy Spirit we can bring the wisdom of the wise up to the higher plane of the foolishness of God. His Spirit will use our limited language to reveal to us His divine ordinances, His commandments, and the knowledge of His being. Then we take our position in God's strategy: We have the outlook from a safe, hidden place.

The foolishness of God can only be understood by faith; the wisdom of men through our senses and intellect. The Bible gives us many clear promises that the Lord leads us and always will lead us: "I will instruct thee and teach thee in the way which thou shalt go: I will guide thee with mine eye" (Ps. 32:8). "And thine ears shall hear a word behind thee, saying, This is the way, walk ye in it, when ye turn to the right hand, and when ye turn to the left" (Isa. 30:21). "And the LORD shall guide thee continually, and satisfy thy soul" (Isa. 58:11).

The Lord leads us through His Word, through feelings, and through circumstances, and mostly through all three together. It is such a wonderful experience when the Lord speaks through our feelings and our thinking when we pray and listen to the Lord. The prayer becomes then a conversation from both sides. We on our side must also learn to expect that the Lord acts according to His promises and leads us on His way. "Obey my voice, and I will be your God, and ye shall be my people: and walk ye in all the ways that I have commanded you, that it may be well unto you" (Jer. 7:23).

The Lord is really a good Shepherd, and a good Shepherd leads His sheep. Nevertheless again and again I hear Christians say that they do not get any guidance. When we do not know the will of the Lord, the cause is often doubt and disobedience.

After my time in the concentration camp all the cruelties of the Gestapo left such an impression on me, and I was so confused, that I said to my friends: "I will work anywhere in the whole world, wherever the Lord sends me, but there is one country where I hope He will never send me, and that is Germany. I never want to hear one word of German again."

That was disobedience. Obedience says: "Yes, Father." Disobedience says: "Yes, but..."

I went to America and there came a shadow over my prayer life. When I asked God for guidance, I did not get any answer. Then I said: "Lord, why is this? I know that you are my good Shepherd, so I must be the cause. Have I been disobedient in any way?" Then the Lord said very clearly: "Germany."

"Then I will go to Germany too, Lord."

As soon as I was willing for this, the light came back to my prayer life. I knew again where the Lord wanted to send me. I received from my good Shepherd direct guidance in the little things of daily life and also for my future plans. You must understand that a "tramp for the Lord," as I am, not only needs guidance for one day, but often for many months ahead, to be able to prepare the working program. I went to Germany later on. After all, the Germans are not my enemies; my best friends live in Germany. But I also found there the enemies who had been so cruel to my sister Betsie and me. But then I have learned a very valuable lesson that when Jesus tells us that we have to love our enemies, He also gives us all the love that He demands from us. In the center of the will of God is rest. Our times are in God's hands: all our wheres, whens, whys, and hows. Although we do not underestimate the power and the urge for destruction of the devil, we have nothing to fear, for we are under the protection of the Victor over all powers of darkness. We experience that we are with Jesus hidden in God. There is nothing better than that. Just as there is quietness and peace in the center of a hurricane, so there is also quietness and peace in the center of the will of God. Yes, with Jesus hidden in God— there is quietness and peace. Then there can be a storm around us, but we are safe.

I have experienced that in America. There was a terrible hurricane, and a thundering roar. Suddenly it was quiet, absolutely quiet. Nothing moved. I asked what had happened. I was told: "Now we are in the center of the hurricane. There is quietness and rest."

So it is when one totally surrenders to the strong hands of Jesus. Then one need not be afraid, even "though the earth be removed, and though the mountains be carried into the midst of the sea" (Ps. 46:2).

God Does Perform Miracles

On my trip to the Far East, I was once in Formosa. The Lord told me very clearly that I had to work in several countries and that I therefore should buy an air ticket. But I had no money. The Lord is not only my Shepherd, He is also my Treasurer and He is very wealthy. Sometimes He tries my faith, but when I am obedient then the money comes just in time. "The cattle upon a thousand hills" belong to Him (Ps. 50:10). Sometimes, when I need money, I say: "Father, I believe that you must sell a cow from the cattle on one of your mountains." And then He answers my prayer.

When I went to the travel agency I said to the girl at the desk: "Will you write down the names of the places for which I need an air ticket? First to Hong Kong, then to Sydney in Australia, Oakland in New Zealand, back again to Sydney, then to Cape Town in South Africa, Tel Aviv in Israel and then to Amsterdam in Holland."

She wrote it down and then asked: "What is your end destination?"

"Heaven."

"How do you write that?"

I spelled "H-E-A-V-E-N."

When she had written it down, she understood what I had said and answered: "Oh, but I do not mean that."

"But I meant it, but you do not need to write it down, because I have already got my ticket."

"How did you receive it?"

"About two thousand years ago there was One who bought my ticket for heaven and I had only to accept it from Him. That was Jesus when at the cross He carried my sins and so made the way to heaven free for me."

A Chinese clerk, who also worked in the agency and had listened to our conversation, passed by. He said: "Yes, that is true."

I asked him: "Have you a reservation in heaven?"

"Yes, I have. I have received Jesus as my Savior and Lord and He has made me a child of God. And a child of God has a place in heaven in the house of the Father."

I said to him: "Brother, will you see to it that this girl will not be too late with her reservation for a place in heaven?"

Then I turned to the girl: "When you do not have a reservation for a seat in a plane, you get into great difficulties, but when you do not have a place in heaven, you will end up in far greater difficulties."

"Brother, you must take care that she is not too late."

Was that a joke? No, I meant it and I mean it also for you who are reading this. Have you made your reservation for a place in heaven? If you are not certain of your salvation, then make a decision now. "As many as received him [Jesus], to them gave he power to become the sons of God" (John 1:12).

When the ticket for the journey was ready, the Lord had given me exactly all the money I needed. Thankfully I looked in the booklet with all the different tickets. Sydney–Oakland–Sydney. But then I saw that not Cape Town followed, but Tel Aviv. And then the tickets were written out for Tel Aviv–Cape Town–Amsterdam. I phoned the travel agency and asked the girl: "Why have you changed my schedule? My Chief has told me that I must go first to Cape Town and after that to Tel Aviv. Now you have changed the sequence, first Tel Aviv and after that Cape Town. God is my Master and I must obey Him."

"But that is impossible," the girl said. "There is not a direct airline from Australia to Africa. There is no island in the Indian Ocean for the plane to land to be refueled. That is why you must first go to Tel Aviv."

"No, I must do what my Chief has told me. Perhaps I must pray for an island in the Indian Ocean. But my schedule has to remain as He had told me."

An hour later the girl phoned: "Did you really pray for an island in the Indian Ocean? I just received a telegram from Qantas, the Australian airline. They have begun to use the Cocos Islands, and now there is a direct route from Australia to Africa, via the Cocos Islands and Mauritius."

"Now you see, Miss, that God does not make mistakes in His plans!"

There is nothing too great for God's power, and nothing too small for His love.

19
Sanctification

"He that is unjust, let him be unjust still: and he which is filthy, let him be filthy still: and he that is righteous, let him be righteous still: and he that is holy, let him be holy still" (Rev. 22:11). These days more than ever before, it is one or the other. The command "Let him be righteous still" is the training, the battle, and the victory in reality, all at the same time and all in view of the coming end-time. Our little "decent" sins are victories for the enemy. That is why we ought to walk very carefully. In this time of preparation—or perhaps we can speak of a breathing space—the longing to get the prophetical armor must be the most serious prayer for the church of believers. What we need for the battle is to be ready and armed. Therefore: Be filled with the Spirit! Fight and bring forth fruit! I cannot help but think of the Israelites who kept

133

their weapons with them when they worked in the fields.

"The fruit of the Spirit is love, joy, peace, longsuffering, gentleness, goodness, faith, meekness, temperance" (Gal. 5:22–23). What an armor! There is not written "fruits," but "fruit." Not like an apple, a pear and a banana, but like several grapes in a bunch. It all belongs together.

He who is filled with the Holy Spirit goes relaxed through life, for he knows that it is not a matter of trying but of trusting, and yielding to Him, "who shall also confirm you unto the end, that ye may be blameless in the day of our Lord Jesus Christ" (1 Cor. 1:8).

It is the Lord Jesus Christ Himself who by His Spirit makes us live sanctified lives, He makes us obedient to what the Bible says:

> But whatever happens, make sure that your everyday life is worthy of the Gospel of Christ. So that whether I do come and see you, or merely hear about you from a distance, I may know that you are standing fast in a united spirit, battling with a single mind for the faith of the Gospel and not caring two straws for your enemies.
>
> Philippians 1:27–28 PHILLIPS

Jesus is Victor! He has conquered Satan, the power of sin, and the world. He that is in you, in me, is Victor! We cannot overcome the enemy. We are powerless in ourselves. We are crucified with Christ, but also resurrected with Him unto a new life, here and now. It is the Lord Himself who accomplishes this. When we know this, we can see God's way, even when we have to go the hard way. "We know that all things work together for good to them that love God" (Rom. 8:28).

It is by the grace of God that we can be conquerors. To be a conqueror, one must allow God to live His life in and through us. Again and again He has to break us; that is to say, He breaks the things in us that protect and maintain "self." We must surrender totally to Him, and let Him do all that is necessary. Thus He gets more and more room in us. He does not want only a part of us, but to fill our whole heart with His power, to fill us more and more with Himself. That means a closer fellowship with Him. That is glory!

The promises in the Book of Revelation are for all overcomers, from the beginning until the end.

And he said unto me, It is done. I am Alpha and Omega, the beginning and the end. I

will give unto him that is athirst of the
fountain of the water of life freely. He that
overcometh shall inherit all things; and I
will be his God, and he shall be my son.

Revelation 21:6–7

When we are totally emptied of ourselves,
we can be full of the Holy Spirit. Then we
are conquerors, and are able to accept all
things from His hand. Besides this, we are
being prepared to inherit all things. "And
every man that hath this hope in him puri-
fieth himself, even as he is pure" (1 John
3:3). The contrasts between the Holy Spirit
and self become more and more acute. But
the Bible has a mighty answer: It is possible to be cleansed. No trying, no striving,
but trusting in Him, looking unto Him in
His Word, in our prayers, in our fellowship
with Him. Then he cleanses us through His
Word, that we bring forth more fruit as a
branch on the vine. Jesus said: "I am the
true vine, and my Father is the husbandman. Every branch in me that beareth not
fruit he taketh away: and every branch that
beareth fruit, he purgeth it, that it may bring
forth more fruit" (John 15:1–2). We cannot direct the knife with which He is going
to purge us. It is to no purpose when we

ourselves cut off a bit here and purge some there. The knife is in His hand, in the hand of the husbandman. He will cleanse and sanctify us.

> The fruit of the Spirit is love, joy, peace, longsuffering, gentleness, goodness, faith, meekness, temperance: against such there is no law. And they that are Christ's have crucified the flesh with the affections and lusts. If we live in the Spirit, let us also walk in the Spirit. Let us not be desirous of vain glory, provoking one another, envying one another.
>
> Galatians 5:22–26

Sanctification is: Being filled with the Holy Spirit!

20
Martyrdom

———— ❧ ————

"But rejoice, inasmuch as ye are partakers of Christ's sufferings; that, when his glory shall be revealed, ye may be glad also with exceeding joy" (1 Peter 4:13). Peter, who himself died as a martyr, tells us in his letters what it means to be one. Perhaps there have never been so many children of God who died as martyrs as in our day. Probably many more will follow. That is said quite clearly in the Book of Revelation.

I remember as a child saying to my father: "I am afraid that I will never be strong enough to die as a martyr."

But he said: "When you have to go on a journey, when do I give you the money for the fare—two weeks before?"

"No, Daddy, on the day I am leaving."

"Precisely, and that is what the Savior does also."

He does not give us grace now for something we may have to pass through later on. If He thinks we are worthy to die as a martyr, He gives us the strength for it at that moment. Once I was in Burundi. A civil war had broken out there. Every day people were imprisoned, including Christians. At night we heard shooting when many were killed. The children of God were in uncertainty. What would the future bring? On Sunday morning I spoke in a church. One could really feel the tension. Who would be arrested this week and killed? Who would be still alive next Sunday?

Then I spoke on 2 Corinthians 4:17, "For our light affliction, which is but for a moment, worketh for us a far more exceeding and eternal weight of glory." I told them of an experience I had gone through myself. It has been recorded in my book *A Prisoner and Yet . . .*

When I was in a concentration camp during the war—Ravensbrück—the Bible was called there "das Lugenbuch" (The Book of Lies). It was a miracle that I still had my Bible. The room in which we lived with seven hundred women was so dirty that we were all full of lice. The guards and the other officers would never enter our room, because they were afraid to get vermin from us. God can use even lice, for that is why I could bring a message of God's Word twice a day.

One day we got a new supervisor whose name was Lony. She was a fellow prisoner, a cruel woman; she told the guards everything we did. One day I opened my Bible. A friend of mine said: "Don't do it today. Lony is sitting behind you. If she knows that you have a Bible, she will see to it that you will be killed in a cruel way." I prayed: "God, give me the strength even now to bring Your Word." He answered that prayer. I read the Bible, brought the message, prayed, and then we sang a hymn: "Commit thy ways unto the Lord." When the song had finished, we heard someone call: "Another song like that!" It was Lony; she had enjoyed the singing. Afterwards I got a chance to explain the gospel to her, to show her the way of salvation. I am not a hero. When you know that what you are saying can mean a cruel death, then every word is as heavy as lead. But I have never had such a joy and peace in my heart as when I gave that message, neither before that time, nor afterwards.

God gave me grace to be a martyr. Now I know from experience that, when God demands it of us, when He thinks we are worthy to be martyrs, He will also give us grace. When I told the church this story, a great joy came into the hearts of these people. Perhaps I must say it was a sad joy. Everyone knew it could be the last time that they were assembled. But I felt as one does when one is at the deathbed of a child of God. Suddenly one sees the things of this world from God's point of view, the light of eternity. It gives a feeling of a certain freedom. One sees the great things great, the small things small. The things that are important in everyday life suddenly become very unimportant.

When a child of God is entering into the presence of the Lord, then one does not ask: "What's the time? When do we have dinner? How much money do we have in hand? What kind of dress shall I wear?" No, all these things fall away; they are no longer important. What, then, is important? The important things are the texts of God's Word, especially those that speak of heaven; for instance, where Jesus says: "In my Father's house are many mansions: if it were not so, I would have told you" (John 14:2).

Important is what is written about the glory of heaven: "O death, where is thy sting?" (1 Cor. 15:55). I thank my God for the victory through Jesus Christ! "While we look not at the things which are seen, but at the things which are not seen: for the things which are seen are temporal; but the things which are not seen are eternal" (2 Cor. 4:18).

I could also tell them that, when we are found worthy to die as martyrs, martyrs' crowns are awaiting us. Eternity is long, but time is short. In that same week, many members of that church were arrested and martyred.

It is necessary, when we prepare ourselves for the end-time, also to be prepared to die for Jesus.

A missionary went back to China. It was still possible then, but very dangerous. Someone asked her: "Are you not afraid to go back?" She said: "There is but one thing I am afraid of, that I would not be willing to be like the grain of wheat that has to die in the ground." Did not Jesus say that following Him means to lose our lives for Him? And that is really to find our lives.

What Does the Word of God Say about Martyrdom?

Beloved, think it not strange concerning the fiery trial which is to try you, as though some strange thing happened unto you:

but rejoice, inasmuch as ye are partakers of Christ's sufferings; that, when his glory shall be revealed, ye may be glad also with exceeding joy.

1 Peter 4:12–13

Only let your conversation be as it becometh the gospel of Christ: that whether I come and see you, or else be absent, I may hear of your affairs, that ye stand fast in one spirit. . . . For unto you it is given in the behalf of Christ, not only to believe on him, but also to suffer for his sake; having the same conflict which ye saw in me, and now hear to be in me.

Philippians 1:27, 29–30

And they overcame him by the blood of the Lamb, and by the word of their testimony; and they loved not their lives unto the death.

Revelation 12:11

Yes, the finished work at the cross of Calvary, the power of the blood of Jesus, is our great victory. We can take this into account in our battle, now and in the future. But the word of our testimony also is a power to gain the victory. We must always be ready to confess the gospel of Jesus Christ before devil and people. If we don't do it, then

there is something wrong. When we are
ready to confess, then we are also ready to
suffer. How is it with you? Are you ready to
tell everyone who is willing to listen? It is
settled for all eternity that Jesus is Victor;
that the whole world belongs to Him!

Also, we must not love our lives unto the
death. In Kampala there is a cross by the
wayside, where once the "martyrs of Kampala" passed by. They were young men,
almost children, who served a very wicked
king about a hundred years ago. He was a
homosexual and wanted to use them. But
these boys were Christians and did not want
this. Then they were warned: "You will be
burned alive." In spite of this threat they
did not want to be guilty of such a sin. So
they were all chained together and had to
walk a long way to the place where they
would be burned alive. As they walked they
sang hymns. They knew: Now we must die,
because we are faithful to Jesus and His
commandments. The Lord gave them grace
and joy! When the chains got mixed up
and they almost fell over each other, they
laughed joyfully. Then one after the other
was burned alive, and when one had his
turn, the others who were waiting for the
same cruel death encouraged him: "Only a

few minutes and then you are with the Lord. We are allowed to do this because we follow Him who carried His cross for us. It is an honor to die as a martyr." They could even sing. Thus the Lord was honored by these awful events. Those fifteen-year-old boys did not love their lives unto the death. The Lord gave them grace for it. He will also give us grace should we be counted worthy to suffer martyrdom.

By His resurrection power the Lord gives us now, and even more so in the end-time, all we need to be strong in Him. "Now I long to know Christ and the power shown by his Resurrection: now I long to share his sufferings, even to die as he died, so that I may perhaps attain, as he did, the resurrection from the dead" (Phil. 3:10 PHILLIPS).

When we die with Jesus, then we also may be resurrected with Him into a new life. By this I do not only mean the resurrection to life after death, but to experience His resurrection power so that "being made comfortable unto his death" can be a reality even now.

In *A Prisoner and Yet . . .* I tell what I once experienced in Ravensbrück. We had to stand for "naked roll call." I never felt so miserable and so ashamed. They took away all our clothing and so we had to stand in the icy cold. I said to my sister Betsie: "This is the very worst thing the enemy has ever done to us. I can hardly bear it." Suddenly I saw Jesus on the cross. The Bible says: "They parted His garments among them." Then I understood through my own experience a little bit of His suffering: He hung naked on the cross for me! When I realized this I understood a little of the ocean of love which Jesus has for us that He carried such a punishment for our sins. That made me so thankful that I was more able to bear my own suffering. When we die with Him, then He also gives us the resurrection power and all the grace we need to live for Him. "But they that wait upon the Lord shall renew their strength" (Isa. 40:31).

God never lets the dominion go out of His hands. When we are in the midst of the battle, sometimes it seems to be one great chaos. Then suddenly the Lord shows us: "I am still here!"

I have experienced this in Africa at a time when the devil had broken loose and so many terrible things were happening. In the newspapers one could read of all sorts of cruelty, but when I listened to what the children of God had to say, I was glad to hear that God had never left His children in Africa alone and that the devil could not go any further than God allowed. We do not always understand this, but some day we shall.

A troop of rebels in the Congo came into a village. The leader asked: "What is that house?"

"That is the house of God."

He took a stone to throw into it, but at that same moment he was killed by a bullet. The bullet must have been misfired by one of his own people. In another village the rebels decided to kill all the Christians. They had come together in a hut to discuss this inhuman plan. At that moment lightning struck the hut and all were killed.

When the rebels advanced on a school where two hundred children of missionaries lived, they planned to kill both children and teachers. In the school they knew of the danger and therefore went to prayer. Their only protection was a fence and a couple of soldiers, while the enemy, who came closer and closer, amounted to several hundred. When the rebels were close by, suddenly something happened: They turned around and ran away! The next day the same thing happened, and again on the third day. One of the rebels was wounded and was brought to the mission hospital. When the doctor was busy dressing his wounds, he asked him: "Why did you not break into the school as you planned?"

"We could not do it. We saw hundreds of soldiers in white uniforms and we became scared." In Africa soldiers never wear white uniforms, so it must have been angels. What a wonderful thing that the Lord can open the eyes of the enemy so that they see angels! We, as children of God, do not need to see them with our human eyes. We have the Bible and faith, and by faith we see invisible things.

In Havana, Cuba, I was once a guest in a boarding school for girls. There were children from two to seventeen years. "May I tell the girls something?" I asked after dinner.

"No, they still have to do all their homework for tomorrow. You may speak for five minutes, no longer!" After four minutes the lights suddenly went out. "Please will you continue until the lights go on again? The children cannot work in the dark!"

I told about all sorts of adventures, my journeys, meetings with children, happy and sad stories. So I was able to tell about the Lord Jesus, who He was and what He is to us in our want and joy. He had said: "Lo, I am with you alway, even unto the end of the world" (Matt. 28:20). After an hour the lights came on again. The children started their home-work. A little girl came to me, put her arms around my neck, and whispered: "I believe that Jesus broke the lights so that you could tell us about Him." In days to come we shall often have to fix our eyes upon the Lord. Often it will seem a lost cause. Often Jesus will have to break the lights, so that we can listen to Him.

In Hong Kong there was a terrible situation among the refugees. So many people came over the border that there was simply no room left. Although the authorities very much regretted this, the frontier had to be closed. Once a day policemen searched the no-man's-land, where the refugees tried to find a hiding place in the mountains and hills. The rest of the day they could move around freely. Now, some missionaries had found out that there was lack of food among these people. They took baskets of bread and drinks and went out to the refugees when the police were not there. They did not only give them food, but also the Bread of Life. Many of these people accepted the Lord Jesus as their Savior. They received a

Bible and a Bible correspondence course. Later many of them were found by the police and sent back to Red China. But also many became real missionaries there. In Hong Kong many letters were received for the Bible correspondence course. So these people were used to bring the gospel to a country where it is impossible for Christians to meet together. So many were in despair, but the angels have rejoiced about what happened. God never makes a mistake! Often we shall have to fix our eyes upon Jesus to see that God has no problems; only plans. There is never a panic in heaven.

21
Jesus Is Victor

The Lord Jesus demands much of us. He said: "For I say unto you, That except your righteousness shall exceed the righteousness of the scribes and Pharisees, ye shall in no case enter into the kingdom of heaven" (Matt. 5:20).

Nowadays people are inclined to belittle God. It is as if they look through the wrong end of a telescope. Their knowledge seems to be unlimited. God is far away and small, for many no longer to be seen. The possibilities for man are indeed unlimited, but only when he does not limit the promises of God through his unbelief. As the mountains and the stars of heaven are unshakable, so the works of Jesus are standing firm as a rock, and even more so, because they bear the stamp of eternity.

Fear not: for I have redeemed thee, I have called thee by thy name; thou art mine. When thou passest through the waters, I will be with thee; and through the rivers, they shall not overflow thee: when thou walkest through the fire, thou shalt not be burned; neither shall the flame kindle upon thee. For I am the LORD thy God, the Holy One of Israel, thy Savior.

Isaiah 43:1–3

The presence of the Lord is our great comfort. With Jesus hidden in God. He invites us: "Abide in me, and I in you." Be strong against a world full of unbelief, without being ashamed for your King. We must be spirit-filled soldiers and must fight to gain the victory, until Jesus comes. He is our strength now, and also in the last battle. "In all these things we win an overwhelming victory through him who has proved his love for us" (Rom. 8:37 PHILLIPS).

Hallelujah!
Jesus was Victor!
Jesus is Victor!
Jesus will be Victor!

He humbled himself by living a life of utter obedience, even to the extent of dying, and the death he died was the death of a common criminal. That is why God has now lifted him so high, and has given him the name beyond all names, so that at the name of Jesus "every knee shall bow," whether in Heaven or earth or under the earth. And that is why, in the end, "every tongue shall confess" that Jesus Christ is the Lord, to the glory of God the Father.

Philippians 2:8–11 PHILLIPS

That is why we stand with Jesus through the Holy Spirit on victory ground. When *you* kneel before Him, will He be your Judge or your Savior?

For God, who commanded the light to shine out of darkness, hath shined in our hearts, to give the light of the knowledge of the glory of God in the face of Jesus Christ.

2 Corinthians 4:6

PART 5

Defeated Enemies

22
The Conflict

Having faced fights not "against people made of flesh and blood, but against persons without bodies—the evil rulers of the unseen world" (Eph. 6:12 LB), in prisons during the war, and later when traveling over the world; and having met so many people—even dear servants of the Lord—who, though surrounded by the powers of darkness, the devil and the demons, do not recognize them, and do not know how to deal with them, I decided, at the request of a missionary friend, to write down what I have learned, as a help for other children of God.

Someone asked my opinion of the missionaries in a certain country. My answer was, "They have given all, but they have not taken all. They have given homeland, time, money, luxury, and more, but they have not taken all the riches abundant that the Word gives us from the boundless resources of God's promises. Many do not know about two precious weapons: the power of the cross and blood of Jesus and every Christian's legal right of the use of the wonderful name of Jesus."

Jessie Penn-Lewis wrote in *War on the Saints*, "When the existence of evil spirits is recognized by the heathen, it is generally looked upon by the missionary as 'superstition' and ignorance; whereas the ignorance is often on the part of the missionary, who is blinded by the prince of the power of the air to the revelation given in the Scriptures, concerning the satanic powers" (21).

We need to recognize the enemy, in order to overcome him. But let us beware of the mistakes that C. S. Lewis describes in *The Screwtape Letters*. He says: "There are two equal and opposite errors into which our race can fall about the devils. One is to disbelieve in their existence, the other is to believe and to feel an unhealthy interest in them! They themselves are equally pleased by both errors, and they hail a materialist or a magician with the same delight" (3).

We have a good safeguard and guide, the Bible, God's Word. Here we find not only the necessary information about Satan and demons, but also the weapons and the armor that we need for this battle, so that, through Jesus Christ, we may be more than conquerors.

Let us keep in mind that God wants and expects us to be conquerors over the powers of darkness—not only for the sake of personal victory, and for the liberation of other souls from the chains of Satan (though this is very important—see Isa. 49:24–25), but for His glory, so that His triumph and victory over His enemies may be demonstrated (Eph. 1:20–23; 3:10; Col. 2:15; 1 John 3:8)!

First, then, let us see what the Bible says about the powers of darkness. The devil or Satan is introduced to us as a person who opposes God and His work (Gen. 3:1). He is the "god of this world," who blinds the minds of the people to the truths of God's Word (2 Cor. 4:4; Eph. 2:2). Having rebelled against God, he was cast out of heaven; then he caused man's fall in paradise. Jesus calls him the father of lies, a liar, a murderer (John 8:44). He works often as an "angel of light" (2 Cor. 11:14), seeking the ruin of the elect! (1 Peter 5:8). But he was cursed of God. Jesus triumphed over him at the cross of Calvary (1 John 3:8) and in His resurrection, and he will finally be condemned and destroyed (Revelation 20). There are many kinds of demons, and they afflict people in various ways (Matt. 12:22; 17:15–18; Luke 13:16). Also, they bring false doctrine (1 Tim. 4:1–4), trying to seduce the elect (Matt. 24:24), oppressing (Acts 10:38), obsessing, and possessing people. They know Jesus, and recognize His power and tremble (Matt. 8:29). For them, hell is the final destination, as it is for Satan.

Secondly, let us consider some references in the Bible concerning the stand we have to take against these powers! It is most important to realize that ours is the position *in Christ*, "far above all principality, and power, and might, and dominion . . ." (Eph. 1:21). We are called to resist the devil (James 4:7) in the whole armor of God (Eph. 6:13–18), by virtue of the blood of Jesus (Rev. 12:11), by faith, prayer, and fasting (Matt. 17:20–21). Jesus cast out demons (Matthew 12), and He commands and expects His disciples to do the same (Matt. 28:20; Mark 16:17; Luke 9–10). In Acts, we learn how the disciples exercised their authority by casting out demons, thus magnifying the name of Jesus (Acts 8:7)!

Let us remember that God's Word stands forever and that His commandments mean for us today exactly the same as for the disciples 2,000 years ago! Those who act on them, in obedience, will in the same way prove God's almighty power. Jesus said, "In my name shall they cast out devils!" (Mark 16:17).

Last of all I want to remind you that your strength must come from the Lord's mighty power within you. Put on all of God's armor so that you will be able to stand safe against all strategies and tricks of Satan. For we are not fighting against people made of flesh and blood, but against persons without bodies—the evil rulers of the unseen world, those mighty satanic beings and great evil princes of darkness who rule this world; and against huge numbers of wicked spirits in the spirit world.

So use every piece of God's armor to resist the enemy whenever he attacks, and when it is all over, you will still be standing up.

But to do this, you will need the strong belt of truth and the breastplate of God's approval. Wear shoes that are able to speed you on as you preach the Good News of peace with God. In every battle you will need faith as your shield to stop the fiery arrows aimed at you by Satan. And you will need the helmet of salvation and the sword of the Spirit—which is the Word of God.

Pray all the time. Ask God for anything in line with the Holy Spirit's wishes. Plead with him, reminding him of your needs, and keep praying earnestly for all Christians everywhere.

Ephesians 6:10–18 LB

Have you heard the name of Pastor Blumhardt? Eighty years ago, in Germany, in a place called Möttlingen, he had to face a grim fight with the powers of darkness. One of his faithful parishioners, Gottliebin Dittus became demon possessed, and a battle started which ended victoriously eighteen months later when the last demon went out of the girl. With a loud voice heard over the whole town, he shouted, "Jesus is victor!" After this, God gave great blessings in Möttlingen. The little town became a center where many Christians received special gifts of healing and of casting out demons (1 Cor. 12:28)!

On his deathbed, Pastor Blumhardt prophesied, "Fifty years from now God will give to Möttlingen a man more gifted than I, and greater things will happen than in my time." This is what happened when Father Stanger started his work and opened "Die Arche," a home where many people found spiritual help, many sick were healed, and many were set free from demon influence. Both of my sisters went yearly to that place and told me much about what they learned. Thus I was not altogether unprepared when I came myself into contact with the powers of darkness.

Now, let me tell you about my own experiences, and how I have proved the wonderful power of the blood of Jesus, and of the name of Jesus, and the trustworthiness of His promises! I have already written down some facts in my books, *A Prisoner and Yet . . .* , *Amazing Love*, *Not Good if Detached*, and so I will add passages from these books that refer to our subject.

There shall not be found among you any one that maketh his son or his daughter to pass through the fire, or that useth divination, or an observer of times, or an enchanter, or a witch, or a charmer, or a consulter with familiar spirits, or a wizard, or a necromancer. For all that do these things are an abomination unto the LORD: and because of these abominations the LORD thy God doth drive them out from before thee. Thou shalt be perfect with the LORD thy God.

> Deuteronomy 18:10–13

After the war in Germany there was among many people great uncertainty about the soldiers that were missing. Were they still in Russian concentration camps, or had they died during the fighting? This uncertainty caused great suffering among their relatives, and many people went to fortune-tellers, to find out about their loved ones. I don't know whether they got any real information, but this I know, many came to me and told me about permanent darkness in their hearts and an urge to commit suicide. This symptom is always a sure evidence of demon influence!

A child of God need not remain in darkness, Jesus said. "I am the light of the world: he that followeth me shall not walk in darkness, but shall have the light of life" (John 8:12).

After I had frequently had such confidences, I decided to speak against the sins of occultism, and so in every series of meetings I spoke once on this subject. I used to read Deuteronomy 18:10–13, showing how these sins are an abomination in the sight of God, because they show how one, instead of depending on His power, asked help from the enemy. Then I showed the help that the Bible gives. It is wonderful that the Bible provides an answer to this serious problem! Jesus came to undo the works of Satan. "God openly displayed to the whole world Christ's triumph at the cross where your sins were all taken away" (Col. 2:15 LB).

In the same way that in 2 Kings 6:5–6 the "son of the prophets" was sent back by Elisha to the place where he had lost the ax and the miracle happened, so I tell people to go back to the place where by their sins they have opened their hearts to the influence of demons, and ask the Lord Jesus to close the door where they have opened it. First, it is necessary to persuade people that they have sinned! Deuteronomy 18:10–13 shows that very clearly. Confession is necessary, and then we may claim the precious promises (1 John 1:7–9) for cleansing. How many I saw liberated instantly when they acted in obedience to this word!

23
Battle against the Powers of Darkness

~~~~~

It is wonderful to have an answer to this problem. Jesus came to undo the works of Satan. The Bible says, "They overcame him [Satan] by the blood of the Lamb, and by the word of their testimony . . . " (Rev. 12:11). Ours is the victory through the blood of the Lamb and the testimony of our witness.

Those that are with us are greater than those that are against us. We need not remain in the dark. Jesus said, "I am the light of the world: he that followeth me shall not walk in darkness, but shall have the light of life" (John 8:12). We possess the authority of His name.

What a joy it was to bring the good news of Jesus' victory into the darkness! But whenever I gave this message, I was so tired I could hardly reach my bed. My heart beat irregularly, and I felt ill.

One evening I had a long talk with my heavenly Father. "I cannot continue like this, dear Lord. Why must I give this message, why must I testify against this particular sin? So many of your faithful servants never mention it! I can't go on like this much longer, and live! Perhaps another month or two, and then my heart will give out!"

Then in the Losungsbuch, a daily devotional book in German, I read, "Be not afraid, but speak, and hold not thy peace: for I am with thee, and no man shall set on thee to hurt thee . . ." (Acts 18:9–10). A short poem follows:

> Though all the powers of hell attack,
> Fear not, Jesus is Victor!

Joy filled my heart. This was God's answer! I prayed, "Lord, I will obey, I will not fear and be silent. But with my hands on this promise I ask you to protect me with your blood, that the demons cannot touch me."

At that moment something happened to my heart; it beat regularly. I knew that I was healed. After this, when having spoken against sorcery and witchcraft, I felt as well

as ever before. Jesus is Victor! The fear of
demons comes from the demons themselves.
We have nothing to fear! He who is with us
is greater than those who are against us! Hidden
with Christ in God; what a refuge! The
mighty High Priest and His legions of angels
are on our side!

Challenge

In my book *Amazing Love* I tell about May,
an intelligent girl in England, who told me
that she longed for peace in her heart, but
always when she would make a decision to
accept Jesus, there was something that kept
her back from this step! I said to her, "Listen,
May. Think back over the events of your life,
and tell me if you have ever been to a fortune-teller.
Do you know that when you do
such a thing you fall under the curse of it, so
that the way to God becomes blocked for you?
Yes, even the way to conversion! Such a spell
may ensnare you even if you have just allowed
yourself to be treated by a mesmerist. Very
often such people are also on the wrong side
and that may be a great danger."

May laughed in a mocking way. "As a
matter of fact, I did allow myself to be persuaded
to go to a fortune-teller years ago,"

she said. "But I did not believe in it, I did it only for fun. Afterwards, we had a real good laugh about it. I had completely forgotten about it, but now, as you ask me, I remember it very well. But surely, there's no harm done, I did not believe it a bit."

"May, suppose you were a soldier during war, and you had to reconnoiter certain terrain. By mistake you fell into the enemy's hands by entering his territory. Do you think that it would help if you then said, 'O excuse me, please, it was not my intention to come here, I just came by mistake'? Once you are on their terrain, you are at their mercy. Though you did not know it, a demon has taken possession of your heart, and your life has fallen under his spell. When you want to be converted, he comes in between. You don't understand the significance of it, and that's why it is so dangerous. Paul says in Ephesians 6:12: 'For we wrestle not against flesh and blood, but against principalities, against powers. . . .'"

The look of amusement had left May's face, and fear was there instead.

"I'm not telling you these things to make you afraid, May. If I had no more to say than this, it would have been better to keep silent, but the first step toward victory is to know the enemy's position. And the wonderful thing about it is that Jesus is victor. *He* is far stronger than all the powers of hell. What you have to do is to close the door exactly where you opened it. I mean this; think of some Scripture passages which speak of forgiveness."

May thought for a moment, and then said, "In whom we have redemption through his blood, even the forgiveness of sins" (Col. 1:14).

"That is right. Now ask the Lord Jesus to go back with you to that very moment when you committed that sin. Confess your sin, ask forgiveness, and give thanks for it, because the text which you quoted is true. Then the door is closed, and you are free. Then you are no longer at the demon's mercy.

"I myself once had the opportunity of showing the way of salvation to a fortune-teller. It was in Germany. The whole day long she was busy 'closing doors.' Then she came back to me and said, 'I feel happier, but I know that there are sins which I have forgotten. I am not completely free yet.'

"'Just tell the Lord Jesus about it as you did me, and give thanks for forgiveness.' I replied.

"Two days later she returned and said, 'This morning I awoke singing. I am completely free.' She was full of praise and thanksgiving to the Lord.

"Will you do it too, May? I know for a certainty that you will be victorious. I'll leave you to yourself now. Fight it out the rest of the way without me."

I left her alone and walked back to the conference grounds. The surf was pounding against the cliffs. A storm was coming up, and it was a tremendous sight. Near the shore a steep rock rose abruptly out of the sea. It was as if two powers fought against each other, but the rock stood unmoved amidst the waves.

On the last night of the conference the leader asked if any would tell what they had learned and experienced these weeks. May stood up and she said, "I have learned and experienced here that Jesus is victor."

A sick woman was sitting in a dirty, messy little kitchen. There was hardly room for my stool. I was eager for a quiet talk with her because she had twice called on a fortune-teller who claimed magic healing power. I told her what a great sin this is in God's sight, because it really means that we run away from God and ask the devil for help. That is why God calls this sin an abomination (Deut. 18:10–12).

A great compassion came into my heart for this woman. I told her about the longing father-heart of God who loves us so much, and who brought us into contact with an ocean of love through Jesus Christ. That is why God thinks it so terrible when we seek help from the enemy.

I noticed that she was now listening attentively. When I warned her earnestly, she defended herself and resisted. Now as I told her with joy about that great love of God, she listened intently. I read to her what Jesus said, "Come unto me, all ye that labor and are heavy laden, and I will give you rest" (Matt. 11:28). Before I left, she prayed and asked forgiveness for going to the fortune-teller, and then she praised and thanked God for the great riches she has in Jesus Christ.

24
Resist the Devil

In a small town in Germany a group of students planned a weekend. Ten Christians each brought an outsider. Though I was the speaker, I felt we were a team, these ten and I! There was much prayer and discussion between the meetings, and when Sunday evening came, eight students had accepted Jesus as their personal Savior!

Trudy, a medical student, followed me that evening as I, tired but grateful, went to my room. "Corrie, thank you so much for all you have done for Heinz. He is my fiancé. He is so different today! Before, he was all gloom; how he is truly happy!"

"What a joy, Trudy! Let us thank the Lord, for He has done it. I am only a branch of the vine, a channel for His blessing. But tell me, Trudy, what about yourself?"

"I haven't come to speak about myself. I wish only to speak about Heinz."

"Just as you like, then we will speak of the great change in Heinz, who has come out of darkness into God's marvelous light."

Suddenly I turned to Trudy and addressed the demons in her. In Jesus' name I bade them leave and go back to hell, where they belong. I saw immediately a great change in Trudy's face. Astounded, she asked, "Is there hope for me?" Then she fell on her knees and cried, "I am free, thank you, Lord, I am free."

With deep joy Trudy praised the Lord, then confessed she had contemplated committing suicide the next day. Looking into her eyes, I could see she was not entirely free, but she left my room praising the Lord. My legs were trembling. I had known nothing about the girl, and all this seemed to have happened outside of myself. What a victory! Though it was late, I went downstairs to find someone to join me in prayer. In the meeting room I found all the students on their knees.

"I've come to tell you that Trudy is free."

"Yes, we know!"

"What do you know? Who told you?"

"We knew she was under the influence of demons. When we saw her go to your room we all knelt in prayer and asked God to use you to deliver her. Suddenly our prayer became praise, and we knew she was free."

"She is not entirely free. Keep on praying for her until she is completely liberated."

Three days later I spoke at the University which Trudy attends, but she hid behind others. The boys asked me to speak to her, but I had not guidance. A week later, she looked me up in a town where I was working, and God used me to finish the work He had begun in her.

I am well aware I do not possess any special gift for casting out demons, but in times of emergency we must dare to lay hold on the promise of Mark 16:17, "In my name shall they cast out devils."

More Than Psychology

Psychology is profitable, even necessary, but not enough. I recall a conversation with a German pastor. It had been a busy and difficult counseling session. Six people had complained about great inner darkness and thoughts of suicide. Some I had been able to help, but not all.

"Can't you help me?" I asked the pastor. "In cases like these, working together is so much better! One can pray, while the other casts out demons."

The pastor answered me with a discourse on the defense mechanism of the sub-conscious. That was no help to me! How dangerous to try to solve great problems with small answers.

A theological professor was asked, "Do you teach your students to cast out demons?"

"Hardly," was the answer. "I can't do that myself."

"But you dare to send your students to congregations that are filled with sorcery? Do you think their knowledge of the Jah-wist and the Elohist manuscripts of Gene-sis will help them when they are struggling with the demons that have entered so many people of our day?"

> Soldiers of Christ, arise,
>   And put your armor on,
> Strong in the strength which God
>   supplies
>   Through His eternal Son;
> Strong in the Lord of hosts
>   And in His mighty power:
> Who in the strength of Jesus trusts
>   Is more than conqueror.
>
> Leave no unguarded place,
>   No weakness of the soul;

Take every virtue, every grace,
  And fortify the whole.
From strength to strength go on,
  Wrestle and fight and pray;
Tread all the powers of darkness down
  And win the well-fought day.
                    Charles Wesley

25
Demon Obsession

There are mental diseases to which men are subject but you can find them described in other books. I will confine myself to speaking of the influence that demons exercise on human beings. E. Flöring, a medical doctor, writes about what she learned:

We can distinguish between demon possession and demon obsession. The distinction refers more or less to the intensity with which demoniac forces have invaded or befallen a person, and with which they stick to that person, or whether they come and go, staying only for certain periods, in between which the person seems to be free and quite normal. According to the number and stickability of the demons, the symptoms of the befallen person will vary from occasional abnormal behavior and subjective abnormal sensations (such as strange voices and thoughts—for example, the urge for murder or suicide, or ever recurring fear of various forms and different types) to more abiding, constant expressions of demoniac character: such as abhorring the name of Jesus, and cursing, and negative reaction when the blood of Jesus is mentioned, and strong dislike of the Bible, expressions of hatred when confronted with the gospel, seemingly unchangeable hardness of heart towards the appeal for repentance, in spite of others' prayers—together with physical symptoms, such as grotesque movements (even dances), strange voices speaking through the person, often with a sound that differs from the person's normal voice, sometimes shrieking; or paralysis of one or more parts of the body, or convulsions and cramps of various kinds, the person sometimes being thrown on the ground. Allergic signs are often present, such as skin alterations, or asthma of various grades of severity. Also, there may be a strange expression of the eyes which looks wild or fearful. Heart sensations of varying character, as well as strong smell, are often found—either one or the other of these symptoms, or more of them combined.

In the prehistory of the person, there has mostly been some connection, either personally or through a member of the family, with witchcraft, or sorcery, or magic (black and white), or fortunetelling, wearing of charms or amulets, or contact with false doctrines, or with persons who exercise demoniac influence, such as witch doctors and medicine men and fortunetellers, or "wise women," or spiritists and radiesthesists, or people who foretell the future from cards or from the lines of one's hand. All these are spiritual influences that make a person's heart receptive to the powers of evil.

Careless dealing with the sin of others, and with demon-befallen persons, can lead to being attacked by demons! Not in vain does Paul exhort Timothy to keep himself diligently.

In practice it may often not be possible to discern between a demon obsession and a demon possession, as the border line cannot be strictly drawn. This does not matter, as far as the method of help is concerned, because the approach to the demon-befallen person will be the same: in the name of Jesus, in the power of His precious blood, by faith and prayer, and, if necessary, fasting, casting out the demons. However, the intensity of the fight will be harder, the enemy more resistant in the case of a possessed person, the battle may last a longer time, until victory is won.

In my own experience, I have heard a demon-possessed human being speaking with a voice different from his own. It can be that a woman speaks with a male voice the moment she is possessed. The expression of the eyes can be terrible! Often demons spread a smell around them! In Berlin, I had to throw open all the windows when a mother who had accepted the Lord as her Savior the day before, brought her demon-possessed daughter to me. After the demons had left the girl, the atmosphere was absolutely clear, the smell had disappeared, along with the demons.

The words "demon possessed" must not be used more frequently than it is actually true! When, for example, someone has to suffer from a difficult mother-in-law, she is often too quickly, and perhaps quite unjustly, described as demon-possessed.

Both demon obsession and demon possession are often the result of occult sin, even those from years ago, and now nearly forgotten, and even entered into "just for fun." This includes contact with hypnotism and all the disobedience spoken of in Deuteronomy 18:10–13. Remember that Gottliebin Dittus was a girl from a Christian home, but had dealt with magic! (See page 162.) And she became possessed by many demons. Her liberation took one and a half years of faithful wrestling and praying by Blumhardt, assisted by many praying Christians. In Matthew 17:21 the Lord Jesus speaks about a kind of demon that "goeth not out but by prayer and fasting."

In Ravensbrück, the prison camp where my sister Betsie and I were in 1944, we had very little to eat. Betsie once said, "Let us dedicate this involuntary fasting to the Lord, that it may become a blessing." After that, we had experiences of victory over the demons around us.

I am so glad that God does not ask us to give a clear diagnosis. We may simply act on His Word, and we experience that God watches over His Word to perform it (Jer. 1:12). What a joy to see an immediate victory through Jesus Christ's power as with the girl in Berlin! Sometimes, the Lord performs the miracle later. In Switzerland, a time of waiting was clearly in God's plan, for it worked out for the opening of the eyes of a minister.

In my book *Amazing Love*, I write:

Callers arrive to see me; a mother and her fifteen-year-old daughter. The child was a pitiful sight, for she cringed in fear at the slightest sound and buried her face in her mother's arm. The mother's face was full of sorrow as she looked at me pleadingly.

"You spoke last night on the reality of the promises of God," she said. "Do you believe that, yourself?"

"Yes, I do," I answered instantly. "God's promises are a greater reality than our problems."

"Then for Christ's sake, cast out this demon," she said vehemently.

I shrank back as though she had struck me. Anything, but not that! That was a terrain on which I did not want to venture. Other people might be able to do so, but not I.

I prayed silently and asked, "Lord, you know that I cannot and will not do this."

The Lord answered me clearly and unmistakably. "But you must do it, because there is even more truth in what you just said to the woman than you yourself realize. My promises are true."

The mother and I read Mark 16, and then we prayed together and asked Jesus Christ to cover us with His blood, and give safe protection in every struggle against, or attack of the devil.

I asked the child, "Do you know the Lord Jesus?"

"Yes, she said, "but I wish He would make me happy. I want to be happy."

Then I spoke to the demon in the name of the Lord Jesus, who has gained the victory on the cross and has cleansed us with His blood. In His name I commanded the demon to come out of the girl and to go back to hell, where he belonged. I forbade him to enter anyone else or to possess the child again.

The poor girl left the manse as much possessed as when she came, and I was profoundly unhappy. How weak I was in faith, and how lacking in power! Was it only theory that I had been preaching, theory that failed when I tried to put it into practice?

I knocked on the door of the minister's study. He received me kindly. "I need your help," I said. "My faith was too small, and now you will have to do it," and I told him about my experience.

He looked up at me, startled, and said, "Oh, that is a sphere I refuse to enter."

"But who must do it then? You are the shepherd of this flock, and you have God's promises. Please read St. Mark 16:17."

He took his Bible and read, "And these signs shall follow them that believe; in my name shall they cast out devils . . ." And verse 20: "And they went forth, and preached everywhere, the Lord working with them, and confirming the word with signs following."

The minister buried his face in his hands. His reading changed to prayer, and I heard him whisper, "Forgive me, Lord, for I have neglected my duty."

Great joy entered my heart. This was the reason I had to experience the failure of my own attempt. This shepherd had to learn something, and God used me as His instrument.

When I left in the evening there was no darkness, but only gratitude in my heart. There was still much that I didn't understand, but everything was all right.

Jesus is Victor.

Two days later I received a letter from the manse.

"Corrie, something wonderful has happened. When the mother and her daughter crossed the threshold of their home the demon went out of the child. This morning both of them came to me full of praise and thanksgiving to Him who was so faithful about the promises He made to us in the Scripture. My husband wants to know if you will come again, and this time stay longer than three days."

But I knew that this would not be necessary. Jesus is Victor, and He uses everyone who is willing to obey Him.

"Whate'er the love of God would do
Is never by His power denied."

Several times I experienced seeming defeat. They are the darkest moments of my
life. I am not called to stay long in one place,
and so I must often stop my efforts too early.
I always hand the cases over to faithful Christians, if they are available. What I always do
in such moments is, that I pray God may
search my heart and show me if somewhere
is an unconfessed sin (Ps. 139:23–24). If we
are disobedient in anything, we ally ourselves
with the enemy! This prayer for heart search-
ing, and—after God has shown us sin—immediately confessing and claiming forgiveness on the grounds of 1 John 1:7–9, is
necessary in every battle with the enemy
where he demonstrates his power in demon-
possessed and demon-obsessed people. We
are on dangerous ground, and anything of
trust in ourselves, love of money, pride, fear,
resentment, or any other sin that blocks the
channel, makes us powerless and must therefore instantly be brought under the cleans-

ing blood of Jesus. This is also absolutely necessary for Christians who assist. Whenever it is possible, I like to be together with another child of God. One can be in prayer during the whole process, while the other deals with the sinner.

26
The Sword of the Spirit

❦

As I said before there is much witchcraft in Germany. One of the forms with which I came in contact was "the letter from Heaven." This contains strange words and sentences, preceded by an introduction that says that the letter comes straight from the Lord Jesus Himself. It promises good luck and protection from danger.

In Berlin I saw an old man in the audience who hungrily listened to my talk. After the meeting I spoke to him and asked, "Did you ever receive Jesus as your Savior?"

"No," was the answer.

"I am sure you want to do it," I said. "I read in your eyes a longing for peace of heart! Jesus can and will give you that, when you ask *Him* to come in. He has knocked at the door, you have heard His voice, and He will come in, when you open your heart. Revelation 3:20 says, 'Behold, I stand at the door, and knock: if any man hear my voice, and open the door, I will come in to him."

"It is not necessary for me," he said. "I have a letter from Heaven!" And he showed me a very old paper; it appeared to be a letter, starting with the words, "I, Jesus, write this letter; it will protect you against every danger." Then followed many words which I could not understand! The man told me, "I tied this paper to a dog during a bombardment in Berlin and sent the dog into the street. The bombs were falling around him, and not one touched him."

"You have to make a choice between this letter and accepting Jesus. This letter is not from Him, but from the devil," I told him.

I looked around and called a girl with a counselor's badge on her dress. I explained the situation to her and said, "Stay with me: one must pray, while the other speaks to this man."

Immediately the girl went to him and quoted by heart the warning words of Deuteronomy 18:10–13. She was a "Navigator" and had followed the Scripture Memorizing Course, and knew immediately how to handle the sword of the Spirit, the Word of God. I saw again how useful it is to know Scripture by heart, thus being prepared for the warfare with Satan! Wherever I go, I see how by this method Christians get practical Bible knowledge! It is used in the campaigns of many evangelists.

I had to leave for the next meeting, so I told the leader of the place about the situation, and advised, "Try to persuade that man to give you the letter for a week. During that time you must try to bring him to the Lord." He did this very thing. First he got in contact with the man, persuaded him to give him the letter, and then showed him the way of salvation. He then accepted the Lord, and wholeheartedly agreed that the letter should be destroyed.

The devil can be a good healer of the body! If he can destroy a soul by healing a body, he is willing to give the temporary blessing of health!

Witchcraft is not only found in heathen lands! I was reading recently of a little girl in Germany who was constantly ill. Someone gave her a charm (amulet), a little box which she had to wear around her neck. Immediately she was healed. Her health was perfect after that, but there was darkness in her heart. She seldom smiled, and at the age of twelve tried to commit suicide. An evangelist was asked to help. He inquired whether perhaps she was wearing some amulet. It took some persuasion before she was willing to hand it over to him, and she said, "Never open it. The one who gave it to me said it would be very dangerous to do so." In spite of this warning, the evangelist opened the amulet and found a little paper, with these words on it, "I command you, Satan, to keep this body healthy, till you get the soul to hell!" They destroyed the amulet and the child was liberated, but instantly became very ill. Later she was healed by the laying on of hands in the name of Jesus.

In Germany, a well-known evangelist had a dreadful experience. A lady came to him in great agony. The expression of her eyes was terrible. The minister had the discernment to see that she was demon-possessed, and in his longing to help her, he laid his hands on her for healing. At the moment when he touched her, he fell backwards on the floor and was unconscious for a whole hour! After recovering, he found that the woman had drowned herself in the river!

When I asked him, "Did you not know that you may never touch a person who is demon-possessed?" he confessed that he had not known that it was dangerous.

Here was a man with a thorough theological training, much Bible knowledge, and a heart full of love to help people, but he failed for lack of knowledge.

Jesus said, "Cast out devils . . . lay hands on the sick" (Mark 16:17–18). He did not say: "Lay hands on the demon-possessed."

We should never deal with people who are under the direct influence of a demon, without claiming the protection or covering of the blood of Jesus! We overcome by the blood of the Lamb (Rev. 12:11). Though we don't understand this, we experience that God meant His promises if we, in obedience, act on the Word of God! The foolishness of God is so much wiser than the wisdom of the wise (1 Corinthians 1–2). Only "faint-knowledge" can grasp these things!

We must also remember that the normal and safe position for every believer is "crucified with Christ" (Rom. 6:6).

If in the conflict with satanic powers the children of God claim the shelter of the blood upon the uncrucified flesh, they remain open to the workings of the spirits of evil.

Mrs. Penn-Lewis writes: "To speak of the blood cleansing the heart from sin and protecting, and not to understand as the cor-relative truth, the believer 'crucified to-gether with Christ,' is failing to apprehend the full power of the work of redemption at Calvary."

How much we need the discernment of the Holy Spirit, that we may discern the spirits and not be fooled! In Matthew 24:24 we read, concerning these last days, "For there shall arise false Christs, and false prophets, and shall show great signs and wonders; insomuch that, if it were possible, they shall deceive the very elect."

The enemy, when he appears as an angel of light, is more dangerous than when he rages as a roaring lion (2 Cor. 11:14)!

A pastor's wife once told me that there was darkness in her soul. She was a dear child of God, knowing that witchcraft sins are an abomination in the sight of God. But once, when she was ill, she consulted a doc-tor in order to find the right treatment. In her absence, he used radiesthesy over sev-eral drugs; he took a ring fastened to a hair and kept it swinging over a drug. When the ring went to and fro, it was to be the right drug, if the ring went round, it was not the right drug. I am not quite sure whether this was the procedure, or whether it worked vice versa. This really does not matter; but it is important that after the minister's wife used the drug thus selected, she came into darkness; so even this subtle use of witchcraft is a great sin.

But Jesus is Victor! *He* liberated her from the darkness. The power of the precious blood and the use of the wonderful name of Jesus were stronger than the power of the enemy. The Christian life is often a battlefield! And the devil has about 6,000 years of experience in laying traps for the saints.

Jesus used the Word. There was nothing complicated about it! He just drew the sword of the Spirit and used it, then the devil left Him, first, for a season (Matthew 4), then fully, until the final scene on Calvary, when all the powers of hell were beaten (Col. 2:15).

27

The Power of Jesus' Name

(Excerpts from *Not Good if Detached*)

───────── ❧ ─────────

"Christ, God's Son, holds [the true child of God] securely and the devil cannot get his hands on him" (1 John 5:18 LB).

How difficult it is to become used to speaking through interpreters! It is like trying to reach people "round the corner." As the listener's eyes are on the interpreter, the speaker is more or less out of touch with his audience. There is, however, one good thing about it—one has time for prayer while speaking!

Today I have an especially fine interpreter. He loves the Lord with all his heart, and it is pure delight to work together—such a contrast to indifferent interpreters! We are guests in the same home, and since we must speak again in the evening, there is time to chat together! Suddenly I ask, "Why is there so much darkness in you?"

"What do you mean?"

"There is no joy of the Lord in your eyes. In the parable of the vine and the branches, the Lord says, 'That my joy might remain in you, and that your joy might be full.' Where is that joy?"

"I don't know!"

"I think perhaps I know! May I speak? When you were converted from Shintoism to the Lord, you turned your back on the demons, but the demons have not turned their back on you!"

In surprise he answers, "That is true! But please don't tell the missionaries. They may think I have gone back to Shintoism."

"Demons are no 'ism.' They are realities as well as angels, and as you, and as I am! You lack a knowledge of the riches that are yours in Jesus! You need not remain in darkness any longer. In the name of Jesus and through the blood of the Lamb we have the victory. In His name you can drive out the demons and withstand Satan."

Together we read and obey the glorious promise and command in Mark 16:15–18, and then the Lord performs the miracle and completely liberates His child.

A few weeks later, we meet again. "Not only am I free," he says, "but my wife and

my children also!" All hail the power of Jesus'
name. His wonderful name is all powerful
in heaven and on earth—that name above
every name!

Many missionaries have given their all—
money, family, and homeland—but they do
not take all the riches offered to them in
God's Word. Theologically their training has
often been basic; but would not a study of
God's Word teach them that to cast out
demons and heal the sick would make them
more fruitful, and should glorify Jesus?

How many dark powers there are in the
world! Yet we have nothing to fear. The fear
of demons is from the demons themselves.
We overcome by the blood of the Lamb, and
His blood protects us. And what joy it is
that we have the authority of the name of
Jesus!

Those who are with us are far more than
those who are against us! At our side is our
mighty High Priest and His legions of angels.

At a conference of Bible school students
it was necessary to have somebody to interpret for me, and this was done by a girl who
found it difficult to understand my English.
When I used an illustration involving radar
in ships, she became quite mixed up, as she
had never heard of radar before! I tried to

help her, and said: "It doesn't matter, we
will try something else. A captain of a ship
stood on a bridge." But she never had heard
of a bridge of a ship, and did not say a word!
I told her, "Read James 1:5, 'If you want to
know what God wants you to do, ask him,
and he will gladly tell you, for he is always
ready to give a bountiful supply of wisdom
to all who ask him; he will not resent it' (LB).
You lack the wisdom to interpret for Corrie
ten Boom, and this is the address where you
can get it!"

But it was too late. She burst into tears.
A Japanese who "loses face" is lost. You cannot do anything with him! I asked the leader
of the conference if there was another interpreter, but he told me there was not! So
here I was, with a message for the young
people before me! Some of them had problems, and the answers could be found in
the Bible that I had in my hand. For what
reason was I unable to bring God's message
to them? Here was the devil at work! The
first step on the way to victory is to recognize the enemy. The devil is a conquered
enemy, and we have the privilege and the
authority to fight him in the name of Jesus!
I turned to the girl and said:

"Dark power, that hinders that girl from interpreting God's message . . . I command you in the name of Jesus to leave her alone! She is meant to be a temple of the Holy Spirit, not your temple!"

As I spoke, the girl was set free! She was able to interpret fluently, and we had a meeting that was greatly blessed. So, what the devil had meant to be an illustration of his victory, became a boomerang and showed the power of Jesus Christ and His name.

Years ago when Dr. Torrey Johnson from the U.S.A. came to Holland to start Youth for Christ work, there was much opposition, and in the newspapers appeared the dirtiest articles about him! Cartoons were printed and the meanest accusations against him were published! When Torrey Johnson arrived, there were no buildings large enough for his meetings. The best advertisement had been made by the enemy! We can learn from such an experience, and we must be careful not to advertise the devil by talking too much about him and his devices!

Some time ago I heard that in India there was a man who had all the symptoms and powers that the Antichrist or his helper will have in the last days! I decided to find out more details to be able to warn more people about him, but when I asked the Lord to guide me and help me to find out, He said, "Don't speak about the Antichrist, speak about Me!" I learned a great lesson! Although we must know and warn each other about the enemy, because lack of knowledge can mean danger, we must not give too much time and words to such warning. The Holy Spirit is on earth to glorify Jesus! We are the temple of the Holy Spirit, and so our task is to be used by Him as channels of streams of living water, for the glorification of Jesus.

"Go ye and teach all nations!" We have a story to tell to the nations, and that is the story of light and love! "We preach Christ . . . the power of God" (1 Cor. 1:23–24).

In South Africa, I received a telephone call, "Corrie, will you help us? There is a demon-possessed girl here and we don't know what to do!"

I was not happy. I have no special gift to cast out demons. Nevertheless I believe that we must never refuse when God calls us! If we don't cast out demons, who must do it? Beelzebub perhaps? Why don't I like it? There is no real fear! Fear of demons is from the demons themselves. But it is always a terrible thing to see a demonstration of the powers of darkness in a human being. I called a friend who had a car, and told her the situation, but she answered, "You know, Corrie, I am always available with my car, but today I can't come! This whole day I must make pies for the church party tomorrow!"

I was angry and put down the receiver. The telephone was in a room where three pastors were visiting. I turned to them and said, "There are too many pies and too many demons in your churches!"

What did I mean? I have nothing against the pies and cakes in the church parties. The only danger for me is that, after some time of working in British countries, there is often "too much Corrie ten Boom," and I have to go on a diet! But how much time is wasted by making the finest and most delicious cakes and pies, when so many people have never heard the gospel! Jesus died for the sins of the whole world, but how many do not know that He died for them?

It can happen that in the house just next to the kitchen, where many hours are spent to bake pies for the church, live people who have a soul to save or be lost for eternity. "Let us redeem the time, the days are evil!"

There are too many demons in our churches! What do people do with a person

who is obsessed or possessed? They go to a
psychiatrist who gives shocks! That means
solving a great problem in a small way, and
that is always dangerous!

One of the pastors took me to the demon-
possessed girl. However, there was defeat
that day! I never understood why! Was there
perhaps anger or resentment in my heart?
That could have been the reason! For if we
give room to any sin, we ally ourselves with
the enemy, and we stand powerless in the
battle!

In New Zealand, I told a group of ladies
who came regularly together for prayer
some of the experiences described in this
book. One said, "Now I understand what is
the matter with my neighbor's little girl! I
fear that she is demon-possessed! Does dis-
tance exist for God, or can we cast out the
demons from here?"

We all went on our knees, and in the
name of Jesus commanded the demons in
the little girl to leave her alone! When the
lady came home, her neighbor came to her
and told her, "My little girl is healed, she is
quite normal." How they rejoiced! But an
hour later, another neighbor came to her
and said, "My little girl has the same dis-
ease as the neighbor's child!"

The lady understood that we had partly failed, because we had not forbidden the demons to go into anyone else! Together with other Christians they cast out the demons from the second child, and told them to go to hell, where they belong!

I am not quite sure whether we may do this last thing. A missionary in Africa told me that this must be said by the Lord Himself! In Jude we read that even the archangel Michael said to the devil: "The Lord rebuke thee" (Jude 9). But since I had that warning I have forbidden the demons in Jesus' name to come back to the same person, or into anyone else, and told them to go to that place to which God commanded them to go. How we need wisdom! But in James 1:5 we read the joyful promise: "If you want to know what God wants you to do, ask him, and he will gladly tell you, for he is always ready to give a bountiful supply of wisdom to all who ask him; he will not resent it" (LB).

What can we ever say to such wonderful things as these? If God is on our side, who can ever be against us? Since he did not spare even his own Son for us but gave him up for us all, won't he also surely give us everything else?

But despite all this, overwhelming victory is ours through Christ who loved us enough to die for us. For I am convinced that nothing can ever separate us from his love. Death can't, and life can't. The angels won't, and all the powers of hell itself cannot keep God's love away. Our fears for today, our worries about tomorrow, or where we are—high above the sky, or in the deepest ocean—nothing will ever be able to separate us from the love of God demonstrated by our Lord Jesus Christ when he died for us.

Romans 8:31–32, 37–39 LB

Corrie ten Boom was imprisoned by the Nazis during World War II for harboring Jews. Upon her release, she began a worldwide ministry of preaching and teaching. *The Hiding Place* is the best-known book about her life.